Our Heritage

OUR HERITAGE:

BRETHREN BELIEFS
AND PRACTICES

A STUDY GUIDE
BY HAROLD H. ETLING

Director Emeritus,
Christian Education Department
of the National Fellowship of Brethren Churches

BMH BOOKS
WINONA LAKE, INDIANA

ISBN: O-88469-022-9

COPYRIGHT 1975
BMH BOOKS
WINONA LAKE, INDIANA

Printed in U.S.A.

All Scripture references in this study guide are from the King James Version
unless otherwise designated.

Pictured on the cover of this study guide is the Germantown Church, home of
the first Brethren congregation in America, formed in 1723. The building is
located In Philadelphia, Pennsylvania. *(Photo by Charles W. Turner)*

DEDICATION

To Ada Marguerite Etling

my faithful wife, and mother
of our two daughters, Lois and Janet

who has been a co-laborer
in the work of Jesus Christ,
Saviour and Lord of each of our lives.

Foreword

BMH Books is delighted to continue this series of Study Guides for the National Fellowship of Brethren Churches. Our primary approach has been to study through the Bible. However, we do desire to select topical studies for a complete balance of curriculum.

This study of Brethren Beliefs and Practices is essential in drawing the attention of our Fellowship to our heritage in history. The fact is emphasized that we accept the Bible to be the foundation for teaching and guidance. A brief historical background is established, and this is followed by study material on our beliefs and practices.

Dr. Harold Etling has done an excellent piece of work in presenting this material. His background suits him well for the assignment. He pastored our Brethren Church in Akron, Ohio, for some years. It was the editor's privilege to be a member of that congregation. Dr. Etling then served for some 18 years as Executive Director of Christian Education in the National Fellowship of Brethren Churches. He presently serves as Conference Coordinator for our Fellowship.

His qualifications in pastoral and executive positions are firmly reflected in this work—Our Heritage.

Charles W. Turner
Executive Editor, BMH Books

TABLE OF
CONTENTS

1. The Infallible Book: The Bible 11

2. So Great Salvation 21

3. The Church 31

   Tunker Fraternity Chart 42

4. Marching Orders of the Church 43

5. Christian Baptism 53

6. The Service of Feet Washing 63

7. The Lord's Supper 73

8. The Bread and the Cup 83

9. The Anointing of the Sick with Oil 93

10. Nonresistance in War and Peace 103

11. Separation from the World 113

12. Consistent in All Things 123

13. The Second Coming of Christ 133

The Infallible Book: The Bible

✳✳✳✳✳✳✳✳✳✳✳✳✳✳✳✳✳✳✳✳✳✳✳✳✳✳✳✳✳✳✳✳✳✳✳✳

CHAPTER ONE

THE CHAPTER OUTLINED:

I. Names of the Bible
   A. The Bible
   B. The Old and New Testaments
   C. The Scriptures
   D. The Word of God

II. Authorship of the Bible
   A. God Is the Author
   B. Man Is the Instrument

III. The Authority of the Bible

IV. The Profit of the Bible

SUGGESTED BACKGROUND DEVOTIONAL READING

Monday—The Holy Scriptures (II Tim. 3:10-17)

Tuesday—A Writer of Scripture (Luke 1:1-4)

Wednesday—Moved by the Holy Spirit (II Peter 1:16-21)

Thursday—All Shall Be Fulfilled (Matt. 5:17-20)

Friday—Faith and the Word of God (Rom. 10:6-17)

Saturday—Scriptures—Perfect and True (Ps. 19:7-14)

Sunday—The Scriptures and the Righteous Man (Ps. 1)

The Bible has been under attack almost from the beginning of time! The Bible is the Word of God, and Satan being aware of this, began to attack the Word in the Garden of Eden. From that moment until the present, Satan has not diminished his efforts. In spite of this continuing assault, the Word of God stands fast, as Jesus promised it would. When He said: "For verily I say unto you, Till heaven and earth pass, one jot or one tittle shall in no wise pass from the law, till all be fulfilled" (Matt. 5:18). Today the Bible is available in more places and in more tongues than ever before in the history of the world. The Bible is the foundation of Christianity, God's revelation to man.

When Sir Walter Scott lay dying he said to those who stood by: "Bring me the Book." To his request they replied, "What book?" Without a moment of hesitation he responded: "There is but one Book. Bring me the Bible." While it is true that "of making many books there is no end," and their number increases daily, yet it is still true there is but one book that deserves the title *the Book,* because this book alone is God's Word to man.

In this age of science, great strides forward have been made. The results are having an impact upon the printing of the words of men, and even upon the printing of the Word of God. There is a system of recordkeeping called electrooptics which has succeeded in reducing letters as much as one million times so that they must be read through a high-powered microscope. This joining of electricity and optics reduced the entire King James Version of the Bible to a slip of plastic one and one-quarter inches square. But even this reduction of the Word to a small bit of plastic does not reduce the truth of God's revelation. The Church has stood through the centuries upon the fact that "God's supreme revelation has been made through Jesus Christ, a complete and authentic record of which revelation is the New Testament: and, to the belief that the Holy Scriptures of the Old and New Testaments, as originally given, are the infallible records of the perfect, final, and authoritative revelation of God's will, altogether sufficient in themselves as a rule of faith and practice" *(The Message of the Brethren Ministry).*

I. NAMES OF THE BIBLE

A portion of the opening sentence of the Epistle to the Hebrews is, "God . . . hath . . . spoken." The question that immediately confronts man is "where?" There are many so-called sacred books of the various religions of the world. In China, the books of Confucianism and Taoism deal with moral problems, but do not claim to reveal things beyond this present earth. In India, the Vedas and other writings comprise a vast literature. In Buddhist countries, they follow the writings of Buddha, while in Mohammedan lands their sacred book is the Koran. But a study of any or all of these writings leaves the student with no assurance of "Thus saith the Lord." It is exactly the opposite with the Bible, for within its pages again and again, there is the assurance that "God . . . hath . . . spoken." Even the names given to it indicate something of the truth of God's revelation to man. Four primary names are used in relation to the Bible.

A. The Bible.

Perhaps the most common of all the names given to our book is "The Bible." The word comes from a Greek word which means "little book." Ancient books were written upon the biblus or papyrus reed, and from this custom came the Greek word "Biblos," which finally came to be applied to our sacred books. (See Mark 12:26; Luke 3:4; Acts 1:20; 7:42). The Bible is not merely a book, but rather it is **The Book**. The Book that from the importance of its subjects, the variety of its content, the majesty of its author, stands as high above all other books as the heaven is high above the earth.

B. The Old and New Testaments.

A second and very common name given to our book is "The Old and New Testaments." (See Luke 22:20; I Cor. 3:6, 14; 11:25; Heb. 9:15; 12:24). The word "testament" means covenant, and is the term by which God was pleased to designate the revelation that existed between himself and His people. The term covenant was first applied to the relation itself, and then to the book which contained the record of that covenant relationship. The Old Testament deals with the record of the calling and history of the Jewish nation, and as such it is the Old Covenant. The New Testament deals with the history and application of the redemption wrought by the Lord Jesus Christ, and as such it is the New Covenant.

C. The Scriptures.

The third name commonly given to the Bible is that of "The Scriptures," sometimes "The Holy Scriptures" (Mark 12:10; 15:28; Luke 4:21; John 2:22; 7:38; Gal. 4:30). These terms mean that the Scriptures are Holy Writings. The early Christians' most common term for the entire Bible was simply, "The Scriptures."

D. The Word of God.

Of all the names given to the Bible, "The Word of God" is doubtless the most significant, impressive, and complete (Mark 7:13; Rom. 10:17; II Cor. 2:17; I Thess. 2:13; Heb. 4:12). This name teaches us to regard the Bible as the utterances of God himself—God speaking to man.

II. AUTHORSHIP OF THE BIBLE

Many people talk about the Bible as God's Word; yet a vast difference is evident in what they mean. Language can be used as a very deceitful instrument, and men often use it to their own advantage. Therefore, it becomes essential that we shall understand that even the words which men use to describe what they are trying to say may be to their own advantage. Because of this, we must define even the words which are used in relation to the Bible, the Word of God.

A. God Is the Author.

The Brethren Church has from its inception held that the Bible is God's Word. This is not the same as saying that the Bible *contains* God's Word. The Bible in its entirety is God's Word and He entrusted it to us. This implies that God has given certain truths which He has determined to reveal to man, and that He has revealed himself to man. This, we call *revelation*. This question of revelation is very current in the thinking of the Christian church. As a matter of fact, Archbishop William Temple writes: "The dominant problem of contemporary religious thought is the problem of revelation—Is there such a thing at all? If there is, what is its mode and form? Is it discoverable in all existing things or only in some? If in some, then in which? And by what principles are these selected as its vehicle? Where is it to be found? What is its authority?"

In answer to the current problems which men are attempting to answer, we believe the Bible has a very fine definition of revelation in Hebrews 1:1 where we read: "God, who at sundry times and in divers manners spake in time past unto the fathers by the prophets."

As we study the Bible, we discover there are a number of ways in which this revelation took place. 1. There was the direct writing of God as is suggested in the giving of the Ten Commandments (Exod. 21:18; 32:16). Concerning this there can be no dispute, and men generally accept this kind of revelation. 2. In addition to this, we discover that sometimes He spoke directly to men (Exod. 33:11). How this was done we do not know, but the Word of God again and again confirms it. This verbal revelation is certainly presented by the voice in the garden, the call of Samuel, the voice from heaven at the baptism of Jesus. 3. Sometimes He revealed himself and that which was to take place through dreams (Gen. 40–41); and 4. closely akin to dreams was the revelation that came through visions (Ezek. 1:1), for an example. 5. In the Book of Psalms, we discover that one type of revelation which God gave to men was through their experiences of life (Ps. 51). 6. The natural events of history became yet another method through which God revealed himself, and He so declares that these are a part of His own revelation (I Cor. 10:6-11). 7. The miraculous events which have come into the history of man have been used of God as still another method of revelation. 8. Finally, there is the direct influence of the Holy Spirit upon the lives of the writers of the Scriptures (II Peter 1:21).

B. Man Is the Instrument (II Tim. 3:14-17).

The second problem of major importance as we face the fact of God's Word is that He used men to give us the Word in written form. In the closing portion of his second letter to Timothy, Paul gave special mention to the books, the parchments—the Scriptures. In the early part of chapter 3 he warned his young son in the faith that godless men would attempt to destroy the truth of the message he was commissioned to proclaim. The opening verses show the character of these men, but Paul left Timothy a good example in his own life, as he pointed out in verses 10-11. In order to remain true during the persecution which was about to fall (v. 12), Timothy was reminded of the true nature of the message he was called to preach.

1. In verse 16 Paul uses a word which appears only on this one occasion in the New Testament. In the King James Version of the Bible, the word is translated "inspiration," and is totally different from the word "revelation." The literal meaning of the word translated "given by inspiration" of God is most accurately translated "God breathed." This then declares that the Bible is the God-breathed Book. This sets it apart from all other books in the world. Every other book in the world came from man, and gives to us man's ideas, his purposes, plans, discoveries, philosophies or imaginations. Many of them have a useful place and function in our social, educational, and civil life. But the Scriptures are in a class by themselves, for they came directly from the mind of God.

2. Inspiration does not blot out human instrumentalities, for God used men to write the Scriptures—actually about forty of them, but these men

were the penmen guided by the Holy Spirit. God did not rob these men of their personalities in their writings, for the human element is recognizable in their works. Moses did not write like Isaiah; David did not write like Peter; nor James like Paul. One must turn to II Peter 1:21 in order to have some insight into the method by which the Bible was given. There Peter writes, "For the prophecy came not in old time by the will of man: but holy men of God spake as they were moved by the Holy Ghost." The men themselves were not inspired or God-breathed, but the word translated "moved" is a very strong word meaning "to be borne or carried forward." The writers had no option as to what they would write. They were driven by an inward compulsion that was irresistible. David indicated this in II Samuel 23:2 when he said, "The Spirit of the Lord spake by me, and his word was in my tongue." Thus could the writers of the Scripture declare, "Thus saith the Lord." The message was not theirs, but His. Often they did not comprehend the full significance of their written messages (I Peter 1:10-11). The inspiration which Paul declared did not involve only thoughts and ideas, but extended to the very words. Gaussen says: "This is the only kind of inspiration that can be." If these men had been left free to choose their own words, what a confusion there would have been! Our Lord himself witnessed to the verbal inspiration of the Scriptures when He said, "Verily I say unto you, Till heaven and earth pass, one jot or one tittle shall in no wise pass from the law, till all be fulfilled" (Matt. 5:18).

3. Only the sixty-six books which comprise the Bible can lay claim to inspiration. No other work has been produced by this enabling ministry of the Holy Spirit, and so the Word of God stands in a category by itself. There are those in the world today who claim that many men have been inspired to write—Shakespeare, Milton, and many others. With these I would have no dispute, for without doubt they were lifted out of themselves when they wrote. But the Bible does not claim merely to be inspired—written by men who were inspired. This one verse—II Timothy 3:16—declares that all Scripture is God-breathed. So our Bible is not simply something that is above the ordinary level of good literature coming from the pen of men who had been lifted out of themselves. This is God's Word, proceeding directly from the mind of God through the channel of the pen of men. It is not man's thoughts about God, but God's revelation of himself, channeled through men whom He chose, and through whom He literally breathed the "very word of God." This means that the Bible in its original autographs is inerrant, which means that it is

without error in all of its parts. Some of the world's best minds have concentrated their attention on the Bible with the sole purpose of discrediting its witness, but it still stands in spite of all attacks.

III. THE AUTHORITY OF THE BIBLE

After we have determined that the Bible is God's Word, the next step is that of authority. Does the Bible have final authority? Is it over and above the church of God? To believe the Bible to be the Word of God is essential to every basic doctrine of the church. To disbelieve the doctrine of the inspiration of the Word of God is to bring to nothingness every other belief. However, is the Bible to become the only rule and authority for the Christian?

This was the basic subject which led to the revolt of Martin Luther against the Roman Catholic Church. The Roman church has maintained, and still does, that Scripture, church, and tradition all share in a triad of authority. The Protestant Reformation, however, stood solidly on the principle that Scripture alone carries divine authority in its words. Luther declared: "For although they [the church fathers] are saintly men, you should not for this reason say they could not err and make mistakes and that we should reply and bank on all the statements they make. But take that touchstone, the divine Word, into your hand, and by it test, evaluate, and judge all that the fathers have written, preached, and spoken and have otherwise set up as rules and human ordinances of any kind. For if we do not do this, we are miserably misled and deceived."

The Brethren Church has through the years held as its motto, "The Bible, the whole Bible, and nothing but the Bible." This means that we accept the Bible as our authority. God through revelation and inspiration has given to us His written Word. Down through these years it has been translated into more than 2,000 languages. This work of the Spirit of God in its original autographs is finished. The second work of the Spirit of God continues until this present moment as He through the written Word makes it vital and meaningful to individuals. Every man who hears or reads the Word of God must choose whether or not he will yield himself to its direction and authority.

IV. THE PROFIT OF THE BIBLE

With the decision of the Supreme Court of the United States that the Bible could not be taught in the public schools as a doctrinal study, much controversy has arisen. However, the Supreme Court of the United States has ruled that the Bible not only may be taught but that it probably should be included in literature and/or history courses as well as studies in comparative religions. It is not our purpose at this moment to enter into the controversy—Rev. W. Arthur Alcorn, of Princeton Theological Seminary, quotes the Court: "One's education is not complete without a study of . . . the Bible" (*The Bible Society Record,* February 1966).

But our purpose is to discover what the Bible says concerning its own value to mankind. Paul in writing to Timothy declares that it is "profitable." Paul uses this word three times in the New Testament. In I Timothy he says that godliness is profitable, in Titus he says that good works are profitable, and in II Timothy 3:16 he says that the Holy Scriptures are profitable.

They are profitable in four distinct areas.

1. The first is "doctrine" (truth, knowledge). The Scriptures do not teach us everything. They do not teach us that we can find gold in a particular mountain, or that Napoleon would lead an army. They were not intended for that purpose. The Scriptures were given to teach us those great truths that man cannot discover for himself, and yet without which he can never know God. One of the foundational doctrines of the Bible is the doctrine of salvation. It is imperative that every person clearly understand his relationship to Jesus Christ before attempting to understand the other great doctrines of the Bible. Timothy knew the necessity of a personal relationship to Christ which is brought about by faith in Him (II Tim. 3:15). As a young man he acknowledged that Jesus Christ died for him, and he trusted in His death to make him acceptable to God, as must be true of every person who has lived from the time of Adam's sin until the present moment (cf. John 3:16).

There are many doctrines which the Bible teaches, including the truth about God the Father, the atoning work of Christ, the indwelling and cleansing power of the Holy Spirit, the depravity of man. In the Bible, God speaks and deals openly with the subject of sin. Sin is always against God, and thus, He never speaks lightly of it. He holds up the Bible as a mirror that we might see ourselves as we really are.

2. The second profitable word is that of "reproof." It is used here in the sense of a rebuke which brings about a conviction of wrongdoing. There are many who have started out to read the Bible with the determined purpose of destroying it. As they have read on through its pages,

they have discovered the Bible pinpointing their own sin. Eventually, through the power of the Holy Spirit, the Word began to work in their hearts and there was a transformation. I do not fear the reading of the Bible or the teaching of it in the public school by unsaved men, for it is the Word of God, and is not going to have any human limitations.

3. Then the Bible is profitable for "correction," to bring man back into the will of God. The word here translated correction has the idea of setting one straight. Every Christian needs this ministry by God's Word, and it should be received as from the hand of the Lord.

4. Finally, the Bible is profitable for "instruction in righteousness." The instruction Paul had in view finds its background in the family circle. It is a word which was used of rearing children. How appropriate it is that as we think of God's Word, we should be reminded that He through this Word instructs us as members of His own family, in righteousness. We are not only saved from sin, but we are redeemed for righteous living. Sin is what is put away; righteousness is the life we live positively.

Now, hear the end of the chapter. Verse 16 does not have a period after "righteousness," therefore, we must note what follows. "That the man of God may be perfect, throughly furnished unto all good works" (v. 17). The Scriptures are inspired, therefore, they are profitable for certain things, but all this is for one great end: that you and I as children of God, born again of His Spirit, may be completely furnished for every good work. If our belief in the Scriptures and the defense of the inspiration of the Word of God do not end in work for Jesus Christ, then our doctrine is dead and we are not what God intended we should be. There is nothing of power in the Word of God that remains unread, nor is there anything powerful in the Word that having been read is disobeyed.

Many years ago, J. Wilbur Chapman gave some advice on Bible study which is still worth following in our generation. He said: "First, study it through. Never begin a day without mastering a verse. Second, pray it in. Never leave your Bible, until the passage becomes a part of your being. Third, put it down. Put the thought God gives you down in the margin of your Bible, or in a notebook. Fourth, work it out. Live the truth you get through all the hours of the day. Fifth, pass it on. Seek to tell somebody what you have learned."

All of the doctrines which we study in the Word are based upon the fact that the Bible is God-breathed. The consequence of this is that the Scripture is infallible. God has preserved over 5,500 handwritten manuscripts of the Old and New Testaments, and thus has insured an accurate and reliable copy of His revelation. Some of these manuscripts are very small, but others contain, for example, the entire New Testament. Not a single doctrine of the New Testament is in doubt. That which is found in our Bible is the message which was written by the writers of Scripture.

So Great Salvation

****

CHAPTER TWO

THE CHAPTER OUTLINED:

I. Salvation — What It Means
    A. Physical Disease
    B. Temporal Danger
    C. Sin and Its Results

II. Salvation — What It Includes
    A. Deliverance from the Wrath and Judgment of God
    B. Deliverance from Sin with Its Evils and Results
    C. Every Spiritual Blessing in Christ
    D. Three Distinct Aspects of Time

III. Salvation — How?
    A. Salvation Is God's Work
    B. Man Must Receive

SUGGESTED BACKGROUND DEVOTIONAL READING

Monday—The Need of New Birth (John 3:1-8)
Tuesday—The Provision of New Birth (John 3:9-18)
Wednesday—Redemption through His Blood (Eph. 1:1-14)
Thursday—Jesus Is the Way (John 14:1-9)
Friday—None Other Name (Acts 4:8-12)
Saturday—How To Be Saved (Acts 16:25-34)
Sunday—Justified Freely by His Grace (Rom. 3:19-26)

Many sat tense as they listened and watched the final efforts of rescue of seventy-eight miners trapped beneath the surface of the earth. Finally, there came the announcement that all hope was gone, the rescue attempt was given up, the mine was sealed off in an attempt to confine the fire that raged beneath. The effort at rescue had been beyond the normal call of duty on the part of those who were involved. It did not lessen the grief of the families and loved ones, nor of those whose sympathies were extended during the days of the attempt to rescue. The words "all hope is gone" are about as dark as can be expressed. What a thrilling thing it would have been, and how the men who made the effort to save them would have been praised, had there been success. Nothing is quite so captivating as a thrilling rescue story. Hence, as we look into God's book for this study, we are involved in the most thrilling story of the universe, the story of God's rescue of the human race from the brink of eternal death.

The theme of this study is from the Word of God, when in Hebrews 2:3 the question is asked, "How shall we escape, if we neglect so great salvation?"

I. SALVATION – WHAT IT MEANS

As we study God's Word, we discover that it sharply distinguishes between two classes of people; namely, "the saved" and "the unsaved"; those "in Christ" and "not in Christ"; the "believer" and the "unbeliever." This distinction is not based upon what may or may not seem reasonable to man, but on the demands and provisions of a righteous and holy God. This distinction must become clear to every student of the Word of God. The truth is that as a church member it is just as terrible to be unsaved, as to be unsaved and not a church member. A teacher of a Sunday School class may be just as lost as the vilest sinner if he has not received Jesus Christ as his personal Saviour. Jesus himself reminded us of this truth in the Sermon on the Mount, particularly in Matthew 7:21-23.

Perhaps as clear a definition as can be found of the word *salvation*, is that given by Webster's Collegiate Dictionary when it says: "The saving of man from the spiritual consequences of sin; especially, deliverance from sin and eternal damnation through the atonement of Christ; redemption." The word in the Old Testament is frequently translated by other words, such as: defend, deliver, help, preserve, rescue, be in health; and in the New Testament: to rescue from danger, to keep safe and sound, to make whole or preserve. Perhaps the best way of explanation of the total meaning of the word as used in the Bible is to turn to several passages which show various uses of the word.

A. Physical Disease.

The first has to do with saving in reference to physical disease. One example is that of Luke 18:42 when Jesus said, "Receive thy sight: thy faith hath saved thee." The words "hath saved thee" actually refer to the physical healing, and might better be translated "thy faith has caused you to see," or "thy faith has cured you."

B. Temporal Danger.

A second usage of the word is that which has to do with salvation from temporal danger, as for example in Acts 27:20 where Luke records, "all hope that we should be saved was then taken away." Paul could not have been referring to anything except hope of physical existence. The storm was so severe that even the most rugged of the sailors was sure the end of the journey had come. Even now, this use of the word is making headlines almost daily in our newspapers and magazines, for the leaders of our nation are urging every citizen who is able to take Red Cross training in life-saving measures to prepare for the day when disaster might come.

C. Sin and Its Results.

But a third usage, and the one with which we are interested in this study has to do with salvation from sin and its results. This is the chief use of the word in the New Testament, and we shall refer to only one passage which describes it for us so perfectly, ". . . thou shalt call his name Jesus: for he shall save his people from their sins" (Matt. 1:21). As we look further at the word we might suggest that from the negative side of the picture, it means to remove or rescue from danger; but on the positive side, it conveys the idea of making a man whole or complete.

II. SALVATION — WHAT IT INCLUDES

Having caught a glimpse of some of the meanings of the word "salvation" as used in the Bible, we must face the next question, "What does Biblical salvation include?" When the Philippian jailer asked the question, ". . . Sirs, what must I do to be saved?"—let us be assured that he had seen the power of God in the lives of the men who were able to sing while in prison, and he had heard the answer to their prayers when the earth rumbled, and the prison doors had opened. This brought fear—the fear of God—into his heart, and now he wanted to be saved. What does that salvation include? His question is not obsolete, nor worn out. It is as real today in our lives as it was nineteen centuries ago in his day.

A. Deliverance from the Wrath and Judgment of God (John 3:17-18; I Thess. 5:9).

In the words of John, the Lord Jesus sets forth His purpose for coming into the world. It was not to reveal God's hatred for men, which would result in their condemnation, but to reveal His love for men by providing a way of salvation, an escape from sin, death, and the grave. He came to save men, but His coming did not automatically secure salvation for all men. While it is true that He did not come to condemn, all those who do not believe in Him remain under condemnation, the condemnation resulting from their sin and transgression. The man who rejects the Christ whom God sent into the world cannot please the Father who sent Him and is thus already condemned.

An American traveler, visiting a famous art gallery in Europe, was shown a famous masterpiece. After viewing the picture rather casually for a moment, he said to the guide, "It doesn't look like so much to me." Whereupon the guide replied, "The picture is not on trial." And so it is with the Lord Jesus—He is not on trial, but men are. When we receive God's gift, salvation includes deliverance from God's wrath and judgment.

B. Deliverance from Sin with Its Evils and Results (Matt. 1:21; Rom. 5:9).

The name given to our Lord at His birth was that which indicated: ". . . he shall save his people from their sins." It is true that the heart cries out to be relieved of the punishment of sin. When man is truly awakened and enlightened by the Spirit of God, he wants to be delivered from the power of evil affections and evil habits, to be saved from his weaknesses and sins, and to be made right with God, and the whole order of things which are of God. This is not the eradication of the old nature, but it is the birth of a new spirit within the man (Ezek. 36:26).

If man is to be saved, not only must he, in the infinite mercy of God, be treated as righteous, but he must actually become righteous, holy, and good. This is the ultimate purpose of God. He removes man's condemnation, He forgives man's sin in order that he may become holy. But man cannot become personally holy until he is set free from the enslaving power of sin. The Saviour of man must deal with this, and He has. How? By the Holy Spirit dwelling and reigning within us. Remember, Jesus

Christ, who saves us from our sins, lives today. He is the one who has all authority. He takes us into union with himself so that it is no longer I that live, "but Christ liveth in me." The man who is in Christ is in Him as the branch is in the vine. So the weakness is turned into might by the coming of His strength into our lives. The sin which strives to enslave the believer finds that it has to deal with the believer's Lord. By the Lord—sin is defeated; its power is broken and its dominion forever overthrown. In Him we conquer sin. His power turns the battle in our favor. Sin has no longer dominion over us. The law of the spirit of life makes us free from the law of sin and death.

C. Every Spiritual Blessing in Christ (Eph. 1:3).

The songwriter once said: "The half cannot be fancied this side the golden shore." As we think of this one verse of the Apostle Paul, we must declare with the songwriter that we cannot imagine that which Christ has accomplished for us. We need to remember that these spiritual blessings become ours the moment we believe in Christ.

Dr. Lewis Sperry Chafer suggests in his book, *Salvation,* that there are at least thirty-three distinct blessings into which the individual is instantly brought by the sufficient operation of the infinite God. Time would forbid the study of all thirty-three, but we dare to at least suggest some of them for your further study. By the finished work of Christ upon the cross, the moment an individual accepts Him as his Saviour, he is made accepted (Eph. 1:6); made the righteousness of God (II Cor. 5:21); made nigh (Eph. 2:13); made sons of God (John 1:21); made citizens of heaven (Phil. 3:20); made a new creation (II Cor. 5:17); made members of the family and household of God (Eph. 2:19; 3:15); made complete in Christ (Col. 2:10); delivered from the power of darkness and translated into the kingdom of God's dear Son (Col. 1:13).

D. Three Distinct Aspects of Time (Rom. 13:11; II Tim. 1:9; I Cor. 1:18).

It is very clear that as far as God is concerned, the moment an individual receives Jesus Christ as Saviour, the transaction is done. As a matter of fact, from Romans, chapter 8, we are sure that God being infinite and omniscient, knew from the beginning each individual who would become a child of His through the work of Christ upon the Cross (Rom. 8:28-39). This passage teaches clearly that salvation includes the transformation from that moment when we were without Christ, and therefore aliens, to the moment when "we shall be like him; for we shall see him as he is" (I

John 3:1-2). We discover three distinct time elements in these passages.

1. The child of God was saved from the guilt of sin and from the penalty of sin, the very moment he believed (past tense). This means that he is both forgiven all trespasses and sins ever committed, and he is justified forever. We read: "Who hath saved us, and called us with an holy calling . . ." (II Tim. 1:9). The man who believes can say, "He hath saved me, and called me." We do not purchase salvation by good behavior or by anything else we can do, but we gain it by what He has done. Now this is the word that refers to our salvation from the guilt and penalty of sin. Paul tells us in Romans 8:1: "There is therefore now no condemnation to them which are in Christ Jesus. . . ." The man who believes is in Christ.

The Bible is full of illustrations of this truth. As Noah and his family were in the ark, hence, saved from the rains and floods, so the Christian is in Christ and is saved from condemnation. As the Children of Israel were safe in the blood-sprinkled house on the night of the Passover, and thus delivered from the terror of physical death, so the Christian is in Christ, and saved from the terror of the Great White Throne of God. Saved by His blood, even as Rahab was safe in the house because of the red thread hung from the window. The scarlet thread of Christ's precious blood gives assurance that since He died, the question of our sin will never be opened again.

2. The child of God is being saved moment by moment from the power and domination of sin (present tense). Perhaps one of the verses that makes this clear is carefully translated: "For the word of the cross is to those who are perishing foolishness, but to us who are being saved, it is the power of God" (I Cor. 1:18 NASV). Norlie, in his translation, puts it thus: "Those on the way to destruction regard the story of the cross as pure nonsense, whereas those of us who are on the way to salvation regard it as the power of God." Let us remember that Satan does not give up his slaves without opposition. The Christian battles daily against every temptation to sin. This is why the Apostle Paul reminds us to "Put on the whole armour of God" (Eph. 6:11). The Christian's past sins are forgiven at the moment he receives Christ as Saviour, and his present sins are likewise under the blood, but we are reminded that the joy of salvation comes as we receive this forgiveness from the Lord through godly sorrow, repentance, and confession (I John 1:8-9). The Christian life is a journey, but we walk only one step at a time. The first step is taken when we receive Christ as Saviour, and then every step along the road is the same—one step at a time, each step trusting Christ completely. We are saved from our sins as we keep our eyes fixed upon the Lord Jesus.

3. A third word concerning salvation is the future aspect when we will be saved from the very presence of sin. This involves "the redemption of our body" (Rom. 8:23) through the resurrection, and the crown of life given to all those who deserve it (Rev. 2:10), and a judgment of the believer's works and rewards. This is the culmination of God's offer to man through Christ, and man's response to this offer. Salvation will not be fully completed until the grave yields up its victims, and the Christian hears the words, "Come, ye blessed of my Father, inherit the kingdom prepared for you from the foundation of the world" (Matt. 25:34).

III. SALVATION — HOW?

As we read the third chapter of the Gospel of John, we are aware that Nicodemus had a real problem. John does not report that Nicodemus ever put into words just what his problem was, yet he came to Jesus with a question in his heart. Jesus began immediately to answer this ruler for we read, "Jesus answered and said unto him, Verily, verily, I say unto thee, Except a man be born again, he cannot see the kingdom of God" (John 3:3). Then came the very important question "How?" It is our question even now. Then Jesus used a very simple illustration to explain why it is difficult to grasp this great truth. Spiritual reality cannot be seen, humanly speaking, any more than the wind that blows can be seen. Men cannot see where the wind comes from, nor where it goes, but they accept it as true because of its effects. Then Nicodemus came back again with almost the same question, "How can these things be?" (John 3:9).

A. Salvation Is God's Work (John 3:14-16).

Having emphasized that every man must be born again, Jesus now teaches that this is possible only because God has provided it through His Son. And although Nicodemus did not realize it then, Jesus was speaking of himself. How?

Jesus reached back into the Old Testament for an illustration when He said, "And as Moses lifted up the serpent in the wilderness, even so must the Son of man be lifted up: That whosoever believeth in him should not perish, but have eternal life" (John 3:14-15). The story of the fiery serpents in the wilderness is recorded in Numbers 21:4-9. As you read again that story, you can sympathize with those who journeyed in the wilderness, for it must have been a long and tedious journey and the people felt worn-out. As a result, they complained about God, because His providence allowed this, and they found fault with Moses because he was leading them in this very difficult hour. As a result of the fault-finding, the judgment of God fell upon them, and fiery serpents were sent in chastisement. The story has a very simple, yet thrilling ending. The people came to Moses and confessed their sin. They asked that the Lord should take the serpents away. He gave them an even greater salvation by providing for life instead of death in the midst of the serpents. A serpent of brass was made and put up high on a pole. When an Israelite was bitten by one of the serpents and was doomed to die because of the poison in the bite, he needed only to look at the brass serpent lifted upon that pole in the center of the camp, and he lived.

Jesus lifted this incident out of its Old Testament setting and applied it here to the salvation which He himself had come to provide. There are other illustrations to which He might have turned: Abraham and his son, Isaac—when in faith Abraham replied, "God will provide himself a lamb . . ." (Gen. 22:8); or Rahab and the story of the scarlet thread; but He used the fiery serpent incident to illustrate and teach that even if a man is truly dead in sin, facing eternal separation from God through all the ages of eternity, he can be saved by a look at the Saviour.

The Bible makes it very clear that "the wages of sin is death," but it is also true that the "gift of God is eternal life through Jesus Christ our Lord" (Rom. 6:23). Salvation is God's work; man is saved on account of Jesus Christ. Paul states specifically in Ephesians 1:7 that it is through the shed blood of Christ that our sins have been forgiven—"In whom we have redemption through his blood, the forgiveness of sins. . . ."

B. Man Must Receive (John 3:18-19).

All that God had provided for the salvation of man is of no avail unless the individual receives that which is offered. The way in which salvation is procured by the unsaved man is, therefore, a matter of great importance. There is a choice to be made, and John tells us about it as he makes the statement: "He that believeth on him is not condemned: but he that believeth not is condemned already, because he hath not believed in the name of the only begotten Son of God" (John 3:18).

This statement is a very simple one that forbids any neutral ground. He that believeth is not condemned, he that believeth not is condemned already. Let us see it very clearly as God has revealed it. An individual is not condemned because he fails to receive Christ. He is already condemned in the sight of God. There is no such thing as any person coming before God with a good record, a clean heart. Every man is a sinner, and is already condemned. Some years ago, a friend of mine in conversation concerning a mutual acquaintance said, "If that man doesn't accept the Lord, he is going to be lost." I quickly responded, "No, he is not *going to be lost,* for the Bible teaches that he is lost *now!*" The individual who has received Christ as Saviour, is lifted out of the realm of condemnation; the man who rejects Christ finds the penalty of sin still there. God has provided a way out of the condemnation which rests upon the human race. The acceptance of this way is the prerogative of every individual. A life preserver will not avail if the man who is sinking in the water refuses to catch hold of it, regardless of how carefully it is thrown to him, how lovingly offered. So it is with Christ and salvation.

When Paul wrote to the Ephesians, he reminded them (Eph. 1:13) that when the Gospel was first presented to the people of Ephesus, they heard the word of truth. But they did more—they believed the message and in believing they were sealed. The believing and the sealing were simultaneous for them as well as for all who trust Christ.

Everyone who becomes a Christian must come in the same manner, for this is the way in which salvation is appropriated. There are four basic facts necessary to receiving Christ as Saviour. (a) There must first be repentance involving a change of mind and direction (Acts 3:19). (b) There must be a recognition of the fact of sin. Salvation is only for sinners, those who have fallen short of God's standard of righteousness. According to the Bible, everyone falls into this category (Rom. 3:23). (c) There is a third recognition, namely, that God has provided a way out of this condition for all mankind. God sent His Son, the Lord Jesus Christ into the world to die for the sin of men. Jesus Christ fulfilled His mission upon the earth by His death on Calvary's cross (John 3:16). (d) But there must be the actual receiving of that finished work by the individual. It is not enough that God made provision for salvation; an individual must accept it as his own, since God will not compel anyone to be saved. The decision must be made on the information given which in Ephesians 1:13 is referred to as "the word of truth." To receive Jesus Christ as Saviour means simply putting complete trust in Christ as the only means of obtaining eternal life.

Why do men then remain under the condemnation? John offers the explanation in John 3:19-20. What John is saying is this: a man who is doing what is wrong does not want the light to shine upon his deeds. Everywhere in the world men commit evil at night when the eyes of other men cannot easily see them. The man who habitually practices evil does not want the light.

Nicodemus had a problem. He came to Jesus, and Jesus looked into the innermost parts of the man, and presented to him the only way out of his dilemma, namely, "Ye must be born again."

God has provided "so great salvation." He has given every individual the privilege, and the responsibility of choosing whether he will accept or reject that gift. No person can take it or leave it as he pleases. It is required of him—of you, that a choice be made, and there is no way to avoid that responsibility.

There may be much here that you do not understand, and may never understand until you reach heaven. But even a child can understand this simple matter of accepting or rejecting Jesus Christ. Faith is the hand of the heart that reaches out and says, "I take." What will you do with Jesus?

The Church

****

CHAPTER THREE

THE CHAPTER OUTLINED:

I. The Meaning of the Church
   A. Popular Concepts
   B. New Testament Concept

II. The Churches

III. The National Fellowship of Brethren Churches

IV. The Purpose of the Church
   A. A Worshiping Church
   B. A Witnessing Church
   C. A Working Church

SUGGESTED BACKGROUND DEVOTIONAL READING

Monday—The Church of Jesus Christ (Matt. 16:13-21)
Tuesday—Holy Spirit Forms Church (Acts 2:41-47)
Wednesday—The Gentiles Included (Acts 10:34, 44-48)
Thursday—The Church Is One Body (Eph. 4:1-6)
Friday—The Church Is a Beloved Bride (Eph. 5:22-33)
Saturday—The Church's Head Is Christ (Col. 1:9-18)
Sunday—Equipped To Serve (I Cor. 12:1-12)

Although there is much talk about the church, and many references to it in the daily publications of men, there is not a corresponding understanding of the church. Church membership in America is at an all-time high. However, over against this fact lies the truth that many church members are very lax in their attendance and support.

The age of which we are a part is an age of triumphs in many fields of endeavor. Because of the advances which have come in the field of science, there is a feeling of unrest among nations and individuals alike. This unrest, which has brought forth new nations and cultures of people has invaded the church, since the church is made up of people.

Because of this changing world, and the unrest among peoples of the world, the church must constantly reflect upon its purpose in the world with reference to the purpose it had in its origin. The church stands or falls by the way it links with its origin in Jesus Christ, and His message; it remains permanently dependent for the ground of its existence on God's saving act in Jesus Christ which is valid for all times—past, present and future. If the church is to make its impact upon the present generation as it has upon generations of the past, then once again, it must be reminded of its original point of reference which must remain as the point of reference in our generation. This point of reference—the original message, is given to us in the writings of the Old and New Testaments. These are the writings which the church itself through several generations, has come to recognize officially as the original, valid and true witness to God's saving activity for man through Jesus Christ.

I. THE MEANING OF THE CHURCH

Too often we take the word *church* for granted, as if everyone knows what we mean when we use the word. It is true that even in church history books the word is seldom, if ever, defined. We confess that very often definitions are difficult to formulate. If, however, we are to talk intelligently, we must be clear as to our meaning.

A. Popular Concepts.

Our search may well begin by a look at some of the popular ideas men have of the church. To some, it is a building. We can point to it, as we do to the store, the bank, or to the school, and say, "There is the church." Even one who never darkens the door of that building may be heard to say, "I pass the church every day on my way to work."

Others see the church existing in the people and the activities which go on within the building. To them the church is like a club or a lodge. It is a group of like-minded people who enjoy the company of each other. They have banded together by their own choice for their mutual benefit and enjoyment. They give money to keep the building in repair. They heat it in the winter and cool it in the summer, and support the various activities. Often a group of churches holding like beliefs and practices will decide to band together uniting their efforts. Such an organization is referred to as a denomination.

Dr. Donald A. Miller in his book *The Nature and Mission of the Church* went so far as to say that there are some who think of the church as "the historic extension of some great past event. It is a society whose purpose is to perpetuate the memory of Jesus or the beginning of the Christian group, much as the DAR rekindles the memory of the American Revolution."

B. New Testament Concept.

If we would understand the truth, we must look to the Word of God for the revelation. The English word *church* comes from the Greek word *kyrakon* which means "that which belongs to the Lord." This word is used only twice in the New Testament, once to designate the Lord's Supper (I Cor. 11:20), and once in speaking of the Lord's Day (Rev. 1:10). Actually, we got the idea from the Scotch word *kirk*. But *church* is especially used to translate another New Testament word which is closely related to the idea of "that which belongs to the Lord." It is the word *ecclesia* from which our word *ecclesiastical* comes, which describes the people who belong to the Lord. This word is one of the favorite words of the New Testament, being used 115 times of which 112 times it is translated as *church* and three times as *assembly*. The word is actually composed of two parts, the first section means "out of," and the latter half means "to call." The context will generally indicate what they have been called out of and what their function is to be.

It is worthy of note that in the New Testament there are three different uses of the word in reference to the Christian church. (a) It refers to the universal church; that is, the entire spiritual body of true Christian believers, regardless of location or time in the dispensation of grace (Eph. 1:22-23; Heb. 12:23). (b) The local church; that is, a local group of professed Christian believers, as in Corinth (I Cor. 1:2, 16:19). (c) The historical church; that is, the whole body of professed Christian believers on earth during a specific or definite period of history. Perhaps the finest picture of this is in the Book of the Revelation, chapters 2 and 3, where there are specific churches named, but each of the churches represents an era of the Christian history as well.

While we are in the midst of the study of the meaning of the church, we do well to remember that the church began its existence on the Day of Pentecost. The description of the birthday of the church is found in the early chapters of the Acts of the Apostles, particularly Acts 1 and 2. It is not to be found in the pages of the Old Testament, for it was not in existence at that time. To talk of the Old Testament Church, or to infer that the Jewish Temple was the church is completely inaccurate and unbiblical.

The church was not in existence during the earthly ministry of the Lord Jesus. He states this when He predicted the formation of the church in Matthew 16:18. The use of the future tense here confirms the truth of this statement.

The church, the body of Christ, is entered by means of the baptism of the Holy Spirit (I Cor. 12:13, Col. 1:24). It is only logical to conclude that the church could not have been in existence before the baptizing ministry of the Holy Spirit was available. According to Acts 1:5, the Holy Spirit's baptism was still future after the resurrection of Christ. Therefore, our conclusion must be that the church was formed and the baptism of the Holy Spirit was initiated in Acts 2:1-4.

There are several pictures given in the New Testament which give at least some of the characteristics of this true church, sometimes called *The Universal Church.*

The church is a *called out body,* and as such is chosen by God, redeemed by Christ, and regenerated and sanctified by the Holy Spirit (I Peter 2:9-10).

The church is a *family,* children of God, heirs of God, and joint heirs with Christ. A large family which transcends all barriers of class, race, and culture (Rom. 8:16-17).

The church is the *bride of Christ.* He loved the church as His bride and gave himself for it. He cherishes it and one day will present it without spot and wrinkle in garments of white (Rev. 19:7-8).

The church is a *building.* It is built on the foundation of Jesus Christ as the chief cornerstone. Believers are the living stones of this spiritual temple (Eph. 2:20-22).

The church is a *forgiven people.* They are cleansed, sanctified, confessing, witnessing, and waiting people (Titus 2:12-14).

The picture which sets forth most completely the nature of the church is the figure of the body, actually called "one body in Christ" (Rom. 12:5-9). This figure of the body receives its fullest expression in I Corinthians 12:12-31. When it is healthy, a human body is a marvelous picture of coordination. Every member in the body has its specific task to do. If a particular member does not do his work, the whole body suffers because of it. The early part of this chapter demonstrates that the Holy Spirit has given a spiritual gift to every believer. The latter verses emphasize that all these different gifts are to function in their rightful places. In other words, there is unity with diversity, and if the body is to perform effectively, there must be coordination of all parts (v. 12).

There is but one condition for membership in this universal church, namely, faith in Jesus Christ. When faith becomes operative in the life of a believer, he receives Christ, and has the prerogatives of the saints of God (John 1:12-13). Without faith no man can justly claim membership in the church which Christ purchased with His own blood. This universal church is invisible to the human eye, but contains the visible church. This church is the body of Christ, but includes the organized body in local churches. This church includes only true believers, both those on earth and those in heaven. The local and historial churches have to do with membership on earth alone, and may include those who are false, as well as the true.

II. THE CHURCHES (Acts 2:41-47; I Tim. 3:1-13)

Early in the record of the New Testament it becomes evident that The Church which is "one body in Christ," manifests itself and exercises its gifts through local churches. These groups of born-again believers, gathered together in a particular locality to worship and serve God, are important to God's plan and program for the extension of the Gospel to the uttermost parts of the earth. Every Christian should be a vital part of his local church.

Acts 2:41-47 outlines the basic requirements for membership in the local church. Verse 41 emphasizes two basic requirements for church membership. These early believers first received the Word which was preached, and then they were baptized. From this beginning of a single local church in Jerusalem, the church continued to grow, but as it did, it attracted attention that soon led to persecution. Persecution scattered the church abroad, and within a matter of a few years, we read of churches in many places. From that moment until the present, the church has made its impact upon the history of the world. In every age, the church has faced numerous foes: paganism of every sort from without, and corruption and power struggles from within. The amazing thing is not that the message and influence of the church were often perverted and even almost lost; the truly amazing fact is that the church has survived in spite of all these things.

Into the pattern of history perhaps the most distinct division came at the time of the Reformation under the leadership of Martin Luther, John Calvin, Huldreich Zwingli and others. The Word of God was restored to its rightful place of sole authority in matters of both Christian doctrine and practice. Justification by faith, once again, became the key emphasis of God's plan of redemption. But within a short time, there settled down upon the Protestant church a barren orthodoxy, and a cold indifference to spiritual things. History records that there was a lack of passion for souls of men, and that the practical side of Christianity had been entirely neglected. Doctrine was well known, but little practiced in life.

III. THE NATIONAL FELLOWSHIP OF BRETHREN CHURCHES

Into the stream of history of the church, in 1708 at Schwarzenau, Germany, there came into being The Brethren Church. For about a quarter of a century, the founders of this church continued to expand the work in Germany until many local congregations had been established. They were given various names indicating some of the particular practices of the group; namely, *Tunkers* because they insisted upon immersion as the only means of baptism; *Dompelaers* because of their forward action in baptism; *Anabaptists* because they belonged to that group of people who rejected infant baptism. They were a Bible-loving, Bible-living, and Bible-preaching group of people.

Persecution forced many of these Brethren out of Germany. They came to the United States of America, and The National Fellowship of Brethren Churches is a continuation of a work that began in 1708 in Schwarzenau. There have been variances of belief through the years causing some cleavage in the ranks (See page 42 for chart of the history of the movements within the framework of the Brethren Church). The emphasis of this group of believers from the beginning, which is maintained until this present hour, is the autonomy of the local church. However, a number of Biblical references imply a wider fellowship than the local church.

New Testament writers show us that churches with like faith shared common interests and means of expression, for we read: "Paul . . . and all the brethren which are with me, unto the churches of Galatia" (Gal. 1:1-3); "John to the seven churches which are in Asia" (Rev. 1:4). New Testament churches, though recognized as local units, were established in the same faith, received the same revelation, and shared in the common needs of all. These facts, by implication at least, provide grounds for the establishment of a fellowship of churches such as our own. In addition to this, it can likewise be said that churches united in common interests can do together what they cannot do alone. This group of churches has continued to stand solidly on congregational government and the refusal to adopt a written creed.

In an attempt to set forth some of the outstanding beliefs, the National Fellowship of Brethren Churches adopted a statement of faith. Because of the importance of this document, we are including it here.

STATEMENT OF FAITH

We of the National Fellowship of Brethren Churches, in harmony with our historic position, believing the Bible, the whole Bible, and nothing but the Bible to be our infallible rule of faith and of practice, and feeling our responsibility to make known the divine message of the Bible, present the following articles as a statement of those basic truths taught in the Bible which are common to our Christian faith and practice:

1. THE BIBLE: The Word of God, the sixty-six Books of the Old and New Testaments, verbally inspired in all parts, and therefore wholly without error as originally given of God (II Tim. 3:16; II Peter 1:21).

2. THE ONE TRUE GOD: existing eternally as three persons—the Father, the Son, and the Holy Spirit (Luke 3:22; Matt. 28:19; II Cor. 13:14).

3. THE LORD JESUS CHRIST: His preexistence and deity (John 1:1-3), incarnation by virgin birth (John 1:14; Matt. 1:18-23), sinless life (Heb. 4:15), substitutionary death (II Cor. 5:21), bodily resurrection (Luke 24:36-43), ascension into heaven and present ministry (Heb. 4:14-16), and coming again (Acts 1:11).

4. THE HOLY SPIRIT: His personality (John 16:7-15); and deity (Acts 5:3-4); and His work in each believer: baptism and indwelling at the moment of regeneration (I Cor. 12:13; Rom. 8:9); and filling (Eph. 5:18) to empower for Christian life and service (Eph. 3:16; Acts 1:8; Gal. 5:22-23).

5. MAN: his direct creation in the image of God (Gen. 1:26-28), his subsequent fall into sin resulting in spiritual death (Gen. 3:1-24; Rom. 5:12), and the necessity of the new birth for his salvation (John 3:3-5).

6. SALVATION: a complete and eternal salvation by God's grace alone, received as the gift of God through personal faith in the Lord Jesus Christ and His finished work (Eph. 2:8-9; Titus 3:5-7; I Peter 1:18-19).

7. THE CHURCH: one true Church, the body and bride of Christ (Eph. 1:22-23; 5:25-32), composed of all true believers of the present age (I Cor. 12:12-13); and the organization of its members in local churches for worship, for edification of believers, and for world-wide gospel witness, each local church being autonomous but cooperating in fellowship and work (Eph. 4:11-16).

8. CHRISTIAN LIFE: a life of righteousness, good works, and separation unto God from the evil ways of the world (Rom. 12:1-2), manifested by speaking the truth (James 5:12), maintaining the sanctity of the home (Eph. 5:22—6:4), settling differences between Christians in accordance with the Word of God (I Cor. 6:1-8), not engaging in carnal strife but showing a Christ-like attitude toward all men (Rom. 12:17-21), exhibiting the fruit of the Spirit (Gal. 5:22-23), and maintaining a life of prayer (Eph. 6:18; Phil. 4:6), including the privilege, when sick, of calling for the elders of the church to pray and to anoint with oil in the name of the Lord (James 5:13-18).

9. ORDINANCES: the Christian should observe the ordinances of our Lord Jesus Christ, which are (1) baptism of believers by trine immersion (Matt. 28:19) and (2) the threefold communion service, consisting of the washing of the saints' feet (John 13:1-17), the Lord's Supper (I Cor. 11:20-22, 33-34; Jude 12), and the communion of the bread and the cup (I Cor. 11:23-26).

10. SATAN: his existence and personality as the great adversary of God and His people (Rev. 12:1-10), his judgment (John 12:31), and final doom (Rev. 20:10).

11. SECOND COMING: the personal, visible, and imminent return of Christ to remove His Church from the earth (I Thess. 4:16-17) before the tribulation (I Thess. 1:10; Rev. 3:10), and afterward to descend with the Church to establish His millennial kingdom upon the earth (Rev. 19:11—20:6).

12. FUTURE LIFE: the conscious existence of the dead (Phil. 1:21-23; Luke 16:19-31), the resurrection of the body (John 5:28-29), the judg-

ment and reward of believers (Rom. 14:10-12; II Cor. 5:10), the judgment and condemnation of unbelievers (Rev. 20:11-15), the eternal life of the saved (John 3:16), and the eternal punishment of the lost (Matt. 25:46; Rev. 20:15).

IV. THE PURPOSE OF THE CHURCH

The purpose of the church as established by our Lord in its institution is best summed up in two passages of Scripture. "As thou [the Father] hast sent me into the world, even so have I also sent them into the world" (John 17:18—note also John 20:21).

At the beginning of the great intercessory prayer of John 17, our Lord declared four things concerning His own ministry that are to be continued through the church. (1) He prayed, ". . . glorify thy Son, that thy Son also may glorify thee," and the mission of the church is to glorify God (I Cor. 6:20). (2) He came to manifest the name of the Father; that is, to declare the truth of God both through lip and life. This continues to be a part of the mission of the church, for we read that the church is ". . . the pillar and ground of the truth" (I Tim. 3:15). Pillars are to uphold the building and the ground is that upon which the pillars are placed. The purpose of the church has been, and continues to be, that of upholding the truth of God. (3) Again, Jesus said, "I have given unto them the words which thou gavest me. . . ." A part of His mission on the earth was to speak forth the Word of God. This has been given to the church as a part of its mission in the world. (4) Finally, He said that He had finished the work He had come to do. The church is to go forth with its face to the future to continue that work.

In order for the church to fulfill the purpose of God, it is essential that the church shall be:

A. A Worshiping Church (Eph. 1:4-6).

We need to remember that at the heart of all religion—pagan, Jewish, or Christian—there is worship. The value of worship depends not upon the sincerity of the worshiper, but rather on the object of that worship. Hence, we read concerning the Early Church, "They continued stedfastly . . . Praising God . . ." (Acts 2:42, 47). The focus of worship must always be the glory of God, not the good of man. One of the purposes in the establishment of the Brethren Church was that of keeping the glory of God uppermost in the hearts and minds of its membership. In modern worship services frequently too much attention is directed toward what happens to the worshiper. All manner of lighting, sound, symbolism, liturgy, and pageantry are utilized to produce emotional feelings in the worshiper. Those who participate tend to evaluate the worship service in terms of how it *lifted them up,* or gave them a *good feeling,* or *inspired them.* It is not God's chief end to glorify man and to make him enjoy himself forever. It is rather man's chief end to glorify God, and to enjoy Him forever.

B. A Witnessing Church (Acts 1:8).

The believers were given a special message—they were to go forth as God's ambassadors to the world. They are under obligation to speak the Word and deliver the message of the Lord. The primary message is the revelation of God in Christ to all men. Again, our church was founded in order that men might band themselves together in a united witness as directed by the Word of God. Members of the Early Church "went every where preaching the word" (Acts 8:4). A quick glance at the growth of the Brethren Church in its early days will show that its members followed this New Testament pattern. God has not called this segment of believers into existence merely to perpetuate something begun in 1708, but rather to be witnesses to Him. Mistakenly, many in this day assume that witnessing is the business of professional workers—pastors, teachers, officers in the church. The church will have much to say about the human soul, and human society, and about our duty in life, but its supreme message is *Jesus Christ; crucified, buried, risen, and coming again.*

C. A Working Church (Acts 2:42-47).

The Word of God makes it very clear that "faith cometh by hearing, and hearing by the word of God" (Rom. 10:17). Hence, we conclude that while salvation does not come by education, it is not apart from education. The Early Church was a teaching church. The Apostle Paul told the church that it should commit to faithful men the truth so that they in turn would be able to teach others. The church of Jesus Christ is not a religious institution with a school attached. It is essentially a school. Christ is the Great Teacher, the Holy Spirit is the interpreter, the Bible is the chief textbook, the pastor is the undershepherd of the school, and around him are gathered teachers and staff. Every church member is an enrolled student, and all others who can be reached are sought as learners to be led toward Christ, and then as they become His children they are urged to become members of the local church.

Another part of the work of the church has to do with serving our fellowmen. The early Christians caught the spirit of Christ, and like Him went about doing good. They performed the ministry of healing the sick, caring for the poor, helping the needy, sharing their goods with one another, comforting the sorrowing, and dealing with the problems of sin and suffering. We dare not bypass this part of our work.

The Brethren Church came into being as a particular church with a particular doctrinal position. Our world calls for the translation of that doctrine into our deeds, and insofar as we continue to practice this, there will continue to be a place for the Brethren Church in God's plan. He will continue to use it and bless it as we continue to remain true to the Bible upon which our church has been founded, not only in doctrine, but also in life.

TUNKER FRATERNITY CHART

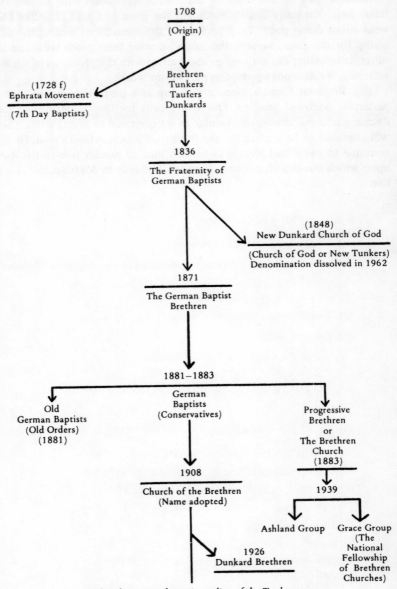

1708
(Origin)

Brethren
Tunkers
Taufers
Dunkards

(1728 f)
Ephrata Movement

(7th Day Baptists)

1836
The Fraternity of
German Baptists

(1848)
New Dunkard Church of God

(Church of God or New Tunkers)
Denomination dissolved in 1962

1871
The German Baptist
Brethren

1881–1883
German
Baptists
(Conservatives)

Old
German Baptists
(Old Orders)
(1881)

Progressive
Brethren
or
The Brethren
Church
(1883)

1908
Church of the Brethren
(Name adopted)

1939

1926
Dunkard Brethren

Ashland Group

Grace Group
(The
National
Fellowship
of Brethren
Churches)

*This chart gives the main outline of the Tunker
development. Some very minor divisions have been omitted.*

Marching Orders
of the Church

****

CHAPTER FOUR

THE CHAPTER OUTLINED:

I. The Brethren Move to America

II. The Beginning of Organized Missions in the Brethren Church
   A. The Foreign Missionary Society
   B. Brethren Home Missions

III. The Brethren Missionary Herald

IV. Grace Schools

V. Sunday School and Youth Ministries

SUGGESTED BACKGROUND DEVOTIONAL READING

Monday—The Church's Commission (Matt. 28:9-20)

Tuesday—Witness of These Things (Luke 24:36-53)

Wednesday—Into All the World (Mark 16:9-20)

Thursday—Power for the Task (Acts 1:6-14)

Friday—A Great Beginning (Acts 2:32-47)

Saturday—Opposition Overcome (Acts 4:23-33)

Sunday—Broadening Horizons (Acts 10:34-48)

It was seemingly a dark day for the disciples when the Lord Jesus was put on the cross, and then later laid in a tomb. Three dark, tragedy-filled days followed, then the Resurrection and the events of the forty days.

As a parting word to the disciples, which subsequently became the marching orders to the Church, Jesus said, "Go ye therefore, and teach all nations, baptizing them in the name of the Father, and of the Son, and of the Holy Ghost: Teaching them to observe all things whatsoever I have commanded you: and, lo, I am with you alway, even unto the end of the world. Amen" (Matt. 28:19-20). Add to this the record of Mark 16:14-18, and the words of Acts 1:8, and you have complete orders. Literally, they say to go tell the Gospel until all have heard. The "Go ye" involves every believer, for He said in Acts 1:8, ". . . ye shall be witnesses unto me . . . ."

The record of the Acts of the Apostles and the various letters to the church give us the picture of the Early Church. We discover an obedience to Christ at the cost of great sacrifice and even of life itself. Obedience to the marching orders of the Lord Jesus has never been cheap. The Early Church suffered persecution and loss in many ways. But they continued to carry the Gospel, beginning in Jerusalem, for we read in Acts 5:42: "And daily in the temple, and in every house, they ceased not to teach and preach Jesus Christ."

Into this stream of the progress of the church the Brethren Church was born. It came into being in response to a great spiritual need. Although the Reformation under the leadership of Martin Luther and his associates, had done much toward restoring the Word of God to its rightful place of sole authority in both doctrine and practice, there broke upon the church a dead formalism and cold indifference to spiritual things. The Reformation had failed to emphasize the practical side of Christianity. Justification by faith had been stressed, but sanctification of life had been neglected. Even Luther himself in his latter years deplored the lack of upright living in the church. In addition to this dead orthodoxy, religious organizations began to be intolerant of each other. In 1648 the Treaty of Westphalia was signed, linking together the Roman Catholic, Lutheran, and Reformed Churches into a persecuting force. These three churches, weary of fighting one another, agreed to tolerate each other, but they denied the right to exist to all others in the German Empire. Thus, though the Peace of Westphalia in 1648 is looked upon as the beginning of the modern denominational development with its allowance of religious liberty, there was much to be desired. Religious liberty was only permitted within prescribed limits.

Prince Henry, of the province of Wittgenstein in western Germany, did not join the other princes of the nation, but allowed full religious freedom to all refugees who sought asylum within his territory. Into this area came many Pietists, Anabaptists, Mystics and others who sought religious freedom. Schwarzenau, Germany, became a center for the discussion and study of matters relating to simple New Testament church doctrine and practice. But once again, it was not long until persecution broke against the church, and with the death of Henry, it became very severe.

In this sheltered vicinity before persecution began to be felt, Alexander Mack (1679-1735), who is usually considered to be the founder of the Brethren Church, and others of kindred spirit met together for prayer and Bible study. The studies of Mack and his associates led them to give adherence to: "The Bible, the whole Bible, and nothing but the Bible." Martin G. Brumbaugh in his book, *A History of the German Baptist Brethren in Europe and America* says: "It will be seen that the new congregation at Schwarzenau studied all denominations; knew all shades of faith and then turned from Ecclesiasticism and Pietism alike to carve out a new and distinct order of faith and practice. They were debtors to all and followers of none" (p. 10 f).

In the year 1708, at Schwarzenau, Germany, straight east of the present city of Cologne, on the Eider River, the Brethren Church came into being. There were eight individuals, five men and three women, who took part in the first baptismal service and thus became charter members of our church. History records that this early group of members had a real missionary spirit, and new members were added to the church regularly. From Schwarzenau, many scattered to other parts of Germany, and other churches were started. Persecution of the church continued, some being robbed of their property, but submitting joyfully. As a result of this, Alexander Mack produced two tracts which set forth his findings from the Scriptures. The first of these, *Ground Searching Questions,* and the other, *A Plain View of the Rites and Ordinances of the House of God.*

I. THE BRETHREN MOVE TO AMERICA

Following this persecution of the Brethren Church in Germany, we discover two waves of emigration to America; one in 1719, and the other in 1729. In addition to these, there were isolated cases of individual Brethren wending their way to the new land. This emigration has been called by Historian Galkenstein "the unique example in history of the emigration of an entire religious denomination." Our intent now is to follow this new group in America in their obedience to the marching orders of the church. How will they and their followers fulfill the command of Christ? We observe them first in their journey across the sea. One brief summary illustration of this group that came in 1719 will suffice. A furious storm arose, which threatened the destruction of the vessel on which they traveled. The sails were lowered and much of the merchandise was thrown overboard. All to no avail. Meanwhile, the Brethren were in their quarters, in the hold of the ship, unitedly pleading with their Heavenly Father. The captain in despair, and directed by Providence, went to the humble compartment of the devoted Tunkers, and behold they were praying and singing! He was impressed with their devotion and serene calmness, and he himself caught the inspiration of hope. He immediately returned to his post and encouraged the crew, declaring that Almighty God would not suffer a ship to perish with such pious people aboard. The storm soon abated, the sea was calmed, and the passage was completed.

Upon arrival in Philadelphia, these people soon scattered, seeking to establish for themselves homes and a livelihood. Into the picture of this early group of Christians, came one by the name of Conrad Beissel, who worked as a weaver. He encouraged the Brethren to do something in the way of uniting their forces, although they were scattered. At this time he himself was not a Brethren, however, he urged them to make a house-to-house canvass of all the families who had been members of the church in Germany. As a result of his urging, in the fall of 1722, three were commissioned to do this labor of love—Peter Becker, John Gomerry, and George Balser Gnasz.

This enterprise has often been called the first home-mission work performed in America by any religious people. The effort was greatly blessed. Some meetings were held in the homes of the believers visited. Brotherly love was stimulated and a desire to do something definite in the way of uniting their forces was realized. The first service of worship was arranged to be held in the home of Peter Becker in Germantown, Pennsylvania. This was actually the first public worship service they had held since their arrival in the New World. Hence, the first service of worship came as a result of house-to-house visitation at least in partial continuance of the direction of Acts 5:42. The next Sunday, they met at the home of John Gomerry, and so every Sunday, alternating from one to the other home, services were held. As a result of many things, a spiritual revival began, and six persons were baptized in 1723. The time was Christmas Day, 1723, with Peter Becker chosen as the baptizer. These six were often referred to as *firstfruits* of Brethren missionary endeavor. Thus, the towns of Schwarzenau and Germantown, and the baptismal streams of Eider and Wissahickon have much the same story to tell. Seventeen Brethren began the work in America.

The first baptismal service was followed by the celebration of the first Love Feast among the Brethren on the continent. There were twenty-three persons now in the group. How did this group fulfill the marching orders of the church? The early history of the Brethren Church records the names of a few men who, because of a deep passion for the souls of others, became the missionaries of the church.

George Wolfe is named as the leader of the Far Western Brethren. He did missionary work over a wide territory for a period of more than thirty-five years. Adam Paine is another who is named as an early missionary, with a real burden for the Indians of northern Illinois and southern Wisconsin.

Jacob Leatherman is another of the pioneer preachers of the Early Church, being known as "the walking preacher." He filled the appointments of five mission points in Maryland for a period of fifty-six years.

With the brief mention of these individuals, we catch something of the spirit of the Early Church (at least some of the members) in obeying the marching orders. From the central states, the church penetrated to the west and north, by means of covered wagon—churches were opened in Iowa, Mississippi, Minnesota, Kansas, Oregon and California. Then followed Nebraska, Washington, Colorado, Texas, Oklahoma, North Dakota and even into Canada.

II. THE BEGINNING OF ORGANIZED MISSIONS IN THE BRETHREN CHURCH

In November of 1892 the general board of missions was incorporated by the Brethren Church, and given the official name of Missionary Board of the Brethren Church. (Let us keep in mind that we are thinking on the great commission to the church—the marching orders of the church. How are these to be carried out? Has the Brethren Church obeyed the Lord?) This board continued to care for the work at both home and foreign missions until at the tenth general conference, held in Winona Lake in 1900, the Foreign Missionary Society of the Brethren Church was born.

A. The Foreign Missionary Society.

It was during this conference in 1900 that Jacob C. Cassel, a prominent elder of the church at that time, presented a paper on the subject, "Are We Ready to Enter the Foreign Missionary Field?" The paper caused a real stir among the Brethren, some receiving it with hearty approval, while others questioned the advisability of putting into effect the proposals of the paper. Some went so far as to voice outright disapproval of any foreign missionary program. But on September 4, 1900, fifty-three members of the church enrolled as members of a new organization known as the Foreign Missionary Society of the Brethren Church.

From this very humble beginning God has blessed the work of this board. For more than twenty-five years the activities of the society were directed from a suite of rooms in the First Brethren Church of Long Beach, California, of which Dr. Louis S. Bauman was pastor. He also served as secretary-treasurer of the society until the year 1946. Then Dr. Russell D. Barnard was chosen to become the first full-time general secretary, with permanent offices established in Winona Lake, Indiana.

From the simple beginning of work in Argentina in 1909, there are now nine fields being served by our missionaries. These include Argentina, Brazil, Central African Republic, Chad, France, Germany, Hawaii, Mexico, and Puerto Rico. At present the total missionary family includes 101 missionaries. There are 13 congregations in Argentina with a membership of 312 persons. The Central African Republic has an approximate church membership of 70,000. The average weekly attendance on this field passes 140,000. In Brazil there are 13 churches with a membership of 514 and a weekly attendance of 846. Mexico has six congregations with a membership of 120, while Hawaii has two churches with a total membership of more than 100. France has eight missionaries and has organized its first church. Rev. John Zielasko is serving as foreign secretary of the society at the present time, and Rev. Raymond Thompson as administrative assistant.

B. Brethren Home Missions.

In the meantime, what has happened to the obedience in relation to the marching orders at home? In 1939 The Brethren Home Missions Council called Rev. R. Paul Miller to be the first secretary of the group, and through his evangelistic fervor and spiritual vision, the work of the council prospered until today more than one hundred new congregations trace their origin to the help that was given them by The Brethren Home Missions Council. Dr. Luther L. Grubb gave many years of leadership to this ministry, which is now under the direction of Dr. Lester Pifer. They seriously took upon their shoulders also the task of carrying the Gospel to other home-mission fields. Currently Home Missions continues to assist two works in Kentucky, one at Clayhole and the other at Dryhill. These works for many years grew under the direction of Rev. and Mrs. Sewell Landrum, Miss Evelyn Fuqua, and Rev. and Mrs. Marvin Lowery. Presently the John Shollys and the Richard Boggs are the missionaries at these two stations.

A work was also begun among the Spanish-speaking people of New Mexico, with the first mission being established at Taos. Rev. and Mrs. Mark E. Malles pioneered this work, followed by Rev. and Mrs. Sam Horney. Under the present leadership of Rev. Robert Salazar, the work at Taos took a step of faith and became a self-supporting church.

A different branch of work was begun in New Mexico under the Home Mission Council in 1947 among the Navajo Indians at Cuba. Rev. and Mrs. Evan Adams were missionaries in this field for many years. Rev. Larry Wedertz is currently serving as the superintendent of the mission.

The Jew has not been neglected in our outreach, for since December of 1949 the Council has shared in the ministry of the Jew in the Fairfax district of Los Angeles, California. Rev. and Mrs. Bruce Button pioneered this work and directed it until the spring of 1969. To indicate how the outreach program is tied together, Bruce Button made his decision to serve among the Jews while at the Brethren Youth Camp held in Winona Lake, Indiana. Rev. and Mrs. John Neely and Miss Isobel Fraser have been greatly used of the Lord in the Jewish work in recent years.

III. THE BRETHREN MISSIONARY HERALD

We are currently living in the age of the printing press. More literature is being printed today than any other time in the history of the world. This brings us to a brief look at the obedience of the Brethren Church through the printed page. It was in the year 1738 that Christopher Sower and his son moved to Germantown, Pennsylvania, and secured a printing press and complete outfit from Germany. This is usually considered to be the press on which was printed the famous Berleberg Bible from 1738 to 1742. These men also produced an annual almanac, and through the efforts of a grandson, the first German hymnbook, the first German newspaper, and the first European Bible published in America. The historical record of the printed page from that moment until the present is one that would fill a book. Weekly papers, tracts, and books by Brethren authors are a part of the outreach ministry. Once again, with the division of 1937-1939 came the incorporation of the Brethren Missionary Herald Company. Dr. Charles Mayes was called to become the first editor, with Dr. J. C. Beal serving as secretary of publications. Under the leadership of Rev. Arnold Kriegbaum, editor and business manager, a new building was completed.

The *Brethren Missionary Herald* magazine is published biweekly. In addition to the magazine, the Herald Company operates BMH Books through which books by Brethren authors are published. Through these and through Sunday School literature, tracts and pamphlets, the Brethren Missionary Herald Company is a part of the great program of obedience to Christ's marching orders. One of the most recent endeavors in the expansion program of the Herald Company is the establishing of a printing plant at Winona Lake. Rev. Charles Turner is Executive Editor and General Manager of the Brethren Missionary Herald Company.

IV. GRACE SCHOOLS

Christopher Sower, the Younger, was instrumental in establishing and sharing in the maintenance of the famous Germantown Academy. With the coming of the Revolutionary War, and the emigrations that followed, the Brethren Church suffered much, especially in the matter of education. Actually, during the days from 1810 to 1850 many Brethren became fearful of education, especially in respect to high schools and colleges. After 1850 several attempts were made to get schools of higher learning started, but most of these failed.

After the division of 1937-1939, students and nearby pastors met in Ashland, Ohio, in the home of Dr. John C. Beal who was then the business manager of the *Brethren Evangelist.* A very memorable prayer service was held in his home seeking divine guidance and direction for the future. Many other prayer meetings were held in Ashland during that summer, and out of them came the formation of the Brethren Biblical Seminary Association. The cordial invitation to begin the seminary in the First Brethren Church of Akron, Ohio, under the able leadership of Dr. Alva J. McClain, was accepted, and Grace Seminary became a reality in the fall of 1937. The school moved to Winona Lake, Indiana, in the fall of 1939 and in 1948 Grace College was founded. There was growth in both college and seminary almost yearly from the day of birth. Dr. Herman A. Hoyt serves as the president of both schools. Every year graduates go forth to serve the

Lord in various fields of service, many finding their way into pastorates and the mission fields of the Brethren Church. The two schools are in the business of preparing young people to carry the Gospel to the uttermost parts of the earth in obedience to the marching orders given by Christ.

V. SUNDAY SCHOOL AND YOUTH MINISTRIES

The Brethren Church has a long history of emphasis upon Sunday School and youth work. Ludwig Hoecker, of Germantown, Pennsylvania, is given credit for organizing within the Brethren Church that which closely approximates the modern Sunday School, and this was forty years before the time of Robert Raikes. Although there was a period from 1810 to 1850 when there was a feeling that Sunday Schools tended toward worldliness, there was a rising tide of interest in the movement. In the first conference of the Brethren Church after the division of 1882-1883, very firm action was taken. The conference passed a resolution favoring Sunday School in general and encouraging the use of all available means toward successfully promoting this work.

A very active Christian Education Department serves the National Fellowship of Brethren Churches. The responsibility of this department is to study and promote the work of Christian education including: Sunday School work, children's church, training hour, Vacation Bible Schools, camps, conferences, retreats, and to recommend or provide literature that will assist the local church to fulfill its responsibility. The department is likewise charged with the study of and assistance with an aggressive program of encouragement and help in establishing and operating Christian Day Schools throughout our Fellowship.

Dr. Harold H. Etling served as director of the department until 1971 at which time Rev. Howard Mayes became director.

Christian Baptism

****

CHAPTER FIVE

THE CHAPTER OUTLINED:

I. The Rite of Christian Baptism

II. Method of Observance of Christian Baptism

III. The Candidates for Christian Baptism

IV. The Purpose and Meaning of Baptism
  A. Baptism Pictures Salvation
  B. Baptism Pictures the Triunity of God
  C. Baptism Pictures the Believer's Union

V. The Practicality of Christian Baptism
  A. Baptism Involves Public Confession
  B. Baptism Involves Personal Consecration

SUGGESTED BACKGROUND DEVOTIONAL READING

Monday—The Great Commission (Matt. 28:16-20)

Tuesday—Belief and Baptism (Mark 16:14-20)

Wednesday—The Word and Baptism (Acts 2:41-47)

Thursday—Believers Baptized in Samaria (Acts 8:1-12)

Friday—Saul of Tarsus Baptized (Acts 9:10-18)

Saturday—Gentile Believers Baptized (Acts 10:34-48)

Sunday—Philippians Baptized (Acts 16:12-15, 25-33)

The Lord Jesus often taught spiritual truths by means of object lessons while He walked upon this earth. Frequently in the choice of these object lessons, He used the things that were closest at hand, and about which people knew most. For example: The disciples came to Him one day with a question, "Who is the greatest in the kingdom of heaven?" Before He began His verbal answer, He set up an object lesson, by calling a little child to Him, and then the story says, ". . . and set him in the midst of them." This accomplished, Jesus was ready to give His answer. You can read this beautiful object lesson in chapter 18 of Matthew, verses 1 through 10.

So the Lord gave to the church two great object lessons, involving four symbols which He commanded should be observed by the church. These have come to be known as ordinances.

The first of these ordinances is that of water baptism, which symbolizes the believer's participation in the death, burial and resurrection of Christ, at the time of the new birth when Christ's redemptive work becomes efficacious.

We shall, in a positive manner, set forth what the Bible teaches about baptism and the interpretation placed upon it by the Brethren Church as we look at the most important passages on the subject.

I. THE RITE OF CHRISTIAN BAPTISM (Matt. 28:19, Mark 16:16)

There are many passages in the New Testament which refer to baptism. We will fall into difficulty the moment we fail to interpret the words in the light of the context in which they were given. For example, in I Corinthians 12:13, the Apostle Paul talks about baptism, but it is very evident that he is referring to spirit baptism. Again, we read that John the Baptist was preaching "the baptism of repentance for the remission of sins" (Luke 3:3). This is the baptism of Old Testament days whereby Gentiles were brought into the program of Judaism.

Christian baptism was something new and different from all other baptisms. It was instituted by the Lord Jesus to be observed by the church throughout the church age. Only two verses give us record of the institution of Christian baptism. One is Mark 16:16, and, although it touches on the matter, it does not give us the commandment or direction for its performance. It is but the statement of a fact.

This then limits us to one verse of Scripture for the institution of the rite; namely, Matthew 28:19. Let us not take this verse out of context. Remember, that at the beginning of the command, Jesus said, "All power is given unto me in heaven and in earth." He is the head of the church, and needs not speak again and again. Once is sufficient. This He did! Now, as subjects of the "Commander-in-chief," "the Head," ours is to obey.

Let us note the four direct words of command given in this one verse, which is actually one command, with four equal parts.

1. There is the command "Go ye." This, when tied together with other passages of Scripture (Mark 16:16; Acts 1:8), demands that the church go to the entire world. For years, the church has accepted the challenge of this passage, and great missionary emphasis has been given around the world.

2. Then there follows the command to "teach." This more literally reads *discipling.* This discipling was to be done through the proclamation of the gospel message. Jesus gave the announcement of this message during the days immediately following His resurrection (Luke 24:46-49). Both Peter and Paul had used this *discipling message,* as they carried the Gospel to the ends of the earth (Acts 2:31-38; 10:39-43; 13:37-39).

3. Now comes the command which is the basis of our present study, which reads, *"baptizing* them in the name of the Father, and of the Son, and of the Holy Ghost."

4. Last, comes the command, "Teaching them to observe all things . . . ." This is just as much a part of the command, and, therefore, a duty laid upon the church as the first "go ye," the *discipling.* The important thing concerning the institution of the rite of Christian baptism is that it cannot be separated from the gospel message, for they are a part of the same command. If the church is duty bound to carry the Gospel to the ends of the world, then it is also duty bound to observe the rite of Christian baptism.

II. METHOD OF OBSERVANCE OF CHRISTIAN BAPTISM (Matt. 28:19; Rom. 6:5)

The Bible is our sole and only authority for baptism, and, likewise, it must be our sole authority for the method used in the observance of Christian baptism. What does it say? The command is very explicit, "baptizing them in the name of the Father, and of the Son, and of the Holy Ghost" (Matt. 28:19). If the translators of our English Bible had translated rather than simply carrying over the Greek letters into the English language, much of the confusion would have never appeared. And we might never have known any problems concerning the method of baptism, for the word *baptizo* is the word *bapto* with the ending *izo* added, thus making it a stronger word. The word *bapto* means "to dip," and is uniformily so translated in the New Testament. *Baptizo* then means "frequent dipping." In fact, according to Liddell and Scott as well as other noted Greek lexicographers, had this verse been translated it would have read, "dipping or immersing them repeatedly." Since immediately following the word *baptism* we find: "in the name of the Father, and of the Son, and of the Holy Ghost," the word to *dip repeatedly* is limited to mean three times.

So, in the formula for baptism (dipping), the Lord was quite specific in that it should be "in the name of the Father, and [in the name] of the Son, and [in the name] of the Holy Ghost." Will not one dipping in all three names answer? Not if we understand the direction of the Lord Jesus. Why? It is shown clearly when we begin to study the meaning of this ordinance.

Is there further direction given? Romans 6:3-5 is a Biblical commentary on the command of the Lord Jesus, for it specifically talks of being baptized in the likeness of His death, and being raised in the newness of life. Verse 5 says, "We have been planted together in the likeness of his death. . . ." Most of us understand that a seed is planted when it is put into the ground and covered over with dirt. So, too, if we have been planted, it means put under water. "In the likeness of his death" needs a bit of study, and for it we turn to John 19:30 where we read, ". . . he [Jesus] bowed his head, and gave up the ghost." When Jesus died, He died with His head bowed forward, thus as we are baptized in the likeness of His death (His head bowed) we are baptized in forward action.

III. THE CANDIDATES FOR CHRISTIAN BAPTISM

Since at least some confusion and divisions have come because of interpretation concerning those "who are the candidates for Christian baptism," we deal with this question before the study of the purpose for baptism. There are those who believe that infants should be baptized, particularly those of the "household of faith," and by this they mean all manner of things. There are those who baptize infants because they believe that baptism has saving merit, and thus all should be baptized even though they are unsaved.

The command of Jesus is very clear on this subject, and we need look no further for evidence as to candidates for baptism. The command clearly states, "baptizing them," and can only refer to those who have been *discipled.* That is, those who have heard the gospel message, have believed in Jesus with their entire heart—literally have turned themselves over to Him. The candidates for baptism were those who were evangelized, converted, and brought within the circle of those who were saved. This immediately rules out infants (babies), for they do not have the ability to believe; the unsaved, for if they have heard, they have not believed. The practice of the church in the beginning is sufficient proof they excluded all who did not believe in the practice of baptism. Sufficient evidence in positive manner is available as we look at only a few passages:

Acts 2:41: "They that gladly received his word were baptized. . . ."

Acts 8:12: "When they believed . . . they were baptized. . . ."

Acts 8:13: "Simon himself believed also; and when he was baptized . . . ."

Acts 8:36-37: ". . . here is water; what doth hinder me to be baptized? . . . If thou believest with all thine heart, thou mayest. . . ."

Acts 16:14-15: ". . . Lydia, . . . whose heart the Lord opened. . . . And when she was baptized . . . ."

Acts 16:32-33: "And they spake unto him the word of the Lord. . . . And [he] was baptized. . . ."

Acts 18:8: "Crispus, . . . believed . . . ; and many of the Corinthians hearing believed, and were baptized."

Acts 19:4-5: ". . . they should believe on him . . . . When they heard this, they were baptized."

IV. THE PURPOSE AND MEANING OF BAPTISM

The order in which the details of the Great Commission were given is quite plain. The apostles were to "go," "to disciple" and then "baptize." In Judaism, baptism was a part of the ceremony by which Gentiles became Jews—often called "Jewish proselytes." They were required by law to repent of their sins, to accept the law as their rule of life, and to indicate the change by discarding their old clothing, submitting to a complete immersion in water, and then the putting on of new garments symbolic of a new life.

Now, Jesus is giving directions for the establishment and extension of His church during the time when He would be gone from them. The "go ye" was plainly set forth when He said to them: ". . . Ye shall be witnesses unto me, both in Jerusalem, and in all Judaea, and in Samaria, and unto the uttermost part of the earth" (Acts 1:8). The message was very plain, *discipling them.* There was to be the message of the *new birth*, whereby God in His infinite mercy and grace introduced divine life into a man—the incoming and abiding of the Holy Spirit without which no one can be a Christian. ". . . If any man have not the spirit of Christ, he is none of his" (Rom. 8:9). The new birth, therefore, results in a thorough cleansing from the sins of the past and a new beginning by the indwelling of the Holy Spirit. The man is made a part of the kingdom of God by the new birth.

To picture this, the Lord Jesus gave us the ordinance of Christian baptism, which is trine immersion in water.

Let us remember that water is good for many things. It is good to drink—and by the drinking, man is able to quench his thirst. It is good for washing the body, clothing, or even a dirty floor. But water cannot wash away sin. If it could, then the death of Christ would not have been necessary. Jesus cried with a loud voice from the cross a word which is translated in our language "finished." Nothing more is essential to salvation, for He purchased salvation for mankind by His death. What water could not do, Christ through His atoning death on the cross accomplished. However, He used water as a symbol. As a matter of fact, water baptism in the Bible is always symbolical. It was true of John's baptism as indicated in Matthew 3:6-11; Luke 3:3, 7-16. It is true in Christian baptism (Rom. 6:3-6).

John said: "I baptize with water . . . but Jesus is he which baptizeth with the Holy Ghost" (John 1:26-34). Here, water baptism is a picture of Spirit baptism. Romans 6:3 tells us that we "were baptized into Jesus Christ," and I Corinthians 12:13, "For by one Spirit are we all baptized into one body. . . ." Both of these speak of a spiritual baptism. The moment we were saved (received Christ as personal Saviour), the Holy Spirit baptized us into Jesus Christ, and into His body, the invisible, universal church. But to picture this baptism, the Lord commanded that we should baptize or immerse. Now, we can do nothing concerning Spirit baptism. That is entirely the work of the Godhead. But we are commanded to baptize believers as the picture of His work.

A. Baptism Pictures Salvation.

Baptism pictures the individual entering into the "body of Christ." Baptism by immersion satisfies the picture of this induction into the body. Anything less than trine immersion spoils the symbolism. Let us ever remember that all three members of the Godhead share in the work of salvation. The Father is the source of it all, and because of His great love,

He sent His Son. He did not spare himself the agony of separation, nor even the agony of seeing His Son die (cf. John 3:16; Rom. 8:32). The Son is the channel and actually accomplished the work of our salvation as He paid the penalty on the cross. The songwriter has put it thus: "He only could unlock the gates of heaven and set us free." The Holy Spirit is the one who convicts and brings us to Christ (I Cor. 12:13).

B. Baptism Pictures the Triunity of God.

Although baptism by trine immersion demands the dipping of the candidate into water three times, it is but "one baptism." Paul reminds us in Ephesians 4:5 that there is "one baptism," and we see this picture as the candidate enters the baptismal waters, and then after baptism comes out again. It is once down into the water and once coming up out of the water, thus signifying but one God. The three dippings, "in the name of the Father, and of the Son, and of the Holy Ghost," picture for us the three distinct persons in the Godhead, while the three equal dippings mark the equality of the three persons.

C. Baptism Pictures the Believer's Union.

This truth is set forth in three distinct ways: 1. The entrance into the water is the picture of the believer's union with Christ in His death (Rom. 6:3). 2. The burial beneath the waters in baptism is the symbol of being buried with Christ (Rom. 6:4). 3. The coming out of the water is the symbol of the new life which we have in Christ Jesus, and of the fact that we should now walk in the newness of life (Rom. 6:4-5).

The reality of the believer's entrance into the church is of course made evident in the fact that he is willing to submit to the ordinance of baptism. Acts 2:41 declares, "Then they that gladly received his word were baptized. . . ." The fact that they had been born again through the power of His Spirit was made evident to those who witnessed it, by their baptism, and immediately upon baptism, they were added to the church. It has been suggested by some that this adding to the church simply means that they were added to the church universal, but the language denies this, for the church is made up of all believers, and no mere professors can slip into this body. However, we discover that in the local church it is possible to baptize one who makes a profession, and later discover he is truly not born again (Acts 8:9-20).

In his booklet, *Triune Immersion in the Light of Scripture and Church History,* James Sweeton sets forth this observation with which we heartily concur: "From the time of the New Testament to the present, the ordinance of baptism has been the first formal and public step identifying the individual with the Christian community. There have been exceptions, but they have always been considered deviations, and usually they were based on the erroneous assumption of the unforgiveableness of post-baptismal sins. The modern 'devaluation' of baptism among certain evangelicals has no doubt been a reaction against the sacramentalism that equates baptism and salvation. But the solution to a problem lies in truth, not in reactionism. It might be argued with some validity that membership in the early Christian community and church membership are not exact equivalents. But the fact remains that Christian baptism is not to occur in the middle, or at the end of the Christian life, but at the outset. . . . Denying the relationship between church membership and baptism only confounds the problem rather than helping to clarify it."

V. THE PRACTICALITY OF CHRISTIAN BAPTISM

We are living in an age when men want everything to be practical. We believe that God is very practical in everything that He has done, and that there are reasons for everything He has commanded man to do. Hence, we look for further light on the matter of the practicality of Christian baptism in water. Why did He ever instruct the disciples to "baptize"? Why not allow people to believe, and be done with it?

A. Baptism Involves Public Confession.

When an individual enters the baptismal waters, he is confessing to all who observe the performance of this step that he is trusting Christ for his salvation from sin. Since salvation is a gift from the Triune God and baptism symbolizes the work of the Trinity, the believer, by entering the waters of baptism, gives public testimony of his utter dependence (Rom. 6:23). Perhaps one of the clearest stories of this is the Ethiopian eunuch found in Acts 8:26-40. By being placed under water, the eunuch was declaring that the sin problem had been dealt with in his life, through the provision of the Lord Jesus on the cross of Calvary. Baptism did not save the eunuch, but it did demonstrate the step of obedience because he had trusted Christ. Paul, in writing to the Romans said, "If thou shalt confess with thy mouth the Lord Jesus, and shalt believe in thine heart that God hath raised him from the dead, thou shalt be saved" (Rom. 10:9). Baptism in water includes a public confession, and is, therefore, a very practical manner of fulfilling this demand of the Word of God.

B. Baptism Involves Personal Consecration (Rom. 6:3-5).

This passage is not primarily dealing with water baptism. The baptism of the Holy Spirit is in view here. However, the outward testimony that the baptism of the Holy Spirit has taken place is seen in the ordinance. Now, as the believer is immersed in water, he is identifying himself in a formal way with Christ and fellow Christians (v. 3). The Christian has been separated from the old life by dying to it, and he is raised to a new life in Christ (v. 4). Water baptism does not accomplish these things, but it does picture them as having taken place.

Human beings are prone to forget. We need to be reminded again and again of that which takes place in life. Hence, we have public wedding ceremonies where two people declare their lives one for the other. This public ceremony causes the parties involved to be reminded of the day they publicly declared their love for each other. So it is with the Christian and the ordinance of baptism. He never can see this rite performed in the church without being reminded of the hour when he went down into the baptismal waters, and there declared his faith in Jesus Christ.

The other practical value is more an objective value in that the picturing of these various truths as suggested in the symbolism of baptism should safeguard the truth itself from being destroyed. For example: the teaching of the three dippings in the water symbolizes the three persons of the Trinity. As long as we practice in truth the trine action, we must hold to the truth that there are three members of the Godhead: Father, Son and Holy Spirit. It would be perfectly possible to practice a trine action, and deny the truth of a Triune God, but it would be a thousand times more difficult to practice this form and deny the truth than to omit the form of a trine action, and deny the same truth.

Church history has revealed to us that often men continue to practice forms after they have discontinued the belief that the form, or rite, teaches—but not for long. We are convinced that one reason there is so much devaluation on the practice of church ordinances in the present hour is because so many have already disbelieved the reality of what they teach. They may not have been bold enough to proclaim it, but they have denied it by their actions.

The rite of trine action immersion will continue to teach through a wonderful visual method that which the Bible teaches as to the Triune God, and the work of each member of the Trinity in our salvation. The attachment of any mysterious saving power to baptism wholly misses the mark. It is a transaction between the saved and the Saviour, and an evidence of a love relationship between the two made public, a pledge "that we might no longer be the slaves of sin" (see Rom. 6:6, *The Epistles of Paul*—W. J. Conybears). It should mark the beginning of a life of service for Christ.

The Service of Feet Washing

****

CHAPTER SIX

THE CHAPTER OUTLINED:

I. The Lord's Love for His Own
   A. In Spite of His Coming Death
   B. In Spite of Their Condition
   C. Unto the Uttermost

II. The Lord Washes His Disciples' Feet
   A. Judas the Traitor
   B. Jesus Washes the Disciples' Feet

III. The Meaning of the Washing
   A. The Necessity of the Washing
   B. The Misunderstanding of Peter
   C. The Explanation of Jesus

IV. The Observance of the Rite Today
   A. "Ought"
   B. "Example"
   C. "Do"

SUGGESTED BACKGROUND DEVOTIONAL READING

Monday—His Hour Was Come (John 13:1-5)
Tuesday—If I Wash Thee Not (John 13:6-11)
Wednesday—Wash One Another's Feet (John 13:12-17)
Thursday—Not All Clean (John 13:18-27)
Friday—If We Confess Our Sins (I John 1:1-10)
Saturday—The Laver of the Word (Eph. 5:25-27)
Sunday—Confessing and Forsaking (Prov. 28:7-14)

There is a Chinese proverb which states that one picture is worth more than ten thousand words. This does not militate against the written or spoken word, but it does place real emphasis upon the value of a picture. The Lord Jesus knew of this value when He instituted the communion service. Included in that first service, came the act of the Lord Jesus, when He stooped down and washed the feet of His disciples.

On a number of occasions throughout the earthly life of our Lord He reminded His family and friends that His hour had not come. However, as we turn to John 13, everything has changed—the time is now here— ". . . his hour was come . . ." (v. 1). He knew everything that lay ahead, every detail of all that was to happen, for He was and is omniscient. Now, we watch carefully and give ear to His words as we discover Him washing the feet of His disciples; then reminding them they will be happy if they follow His direction and example and wash one another's feet.

Some very simple items of the physical world are all the properties needed to make this picture one of real teaching as well as a picture that will long be remembered. There was His own garment, which He laid aside; a pitcher filled with water, a basin, and a towel. All are items of the average household, but He used them to teach and to demonstrate to His disciples. In this way our Lord established an ordinance of the communion service, such as we have here.

I. THE LORD'S LOVE FOR HIS OWN (John 13:1)

It was Tuesday evening, just preceding the crucifixion, that the Lord met with His disciples in an upper room. The Apostle John very carefully states that it was "before the feast of the passover . . ." (v. 1). We have suggested in the previous chapter, that the time is therefore established. This becomes very important in the matter of determining the time of His death, for He had said: "Destroy this temple, and in three days I will raise it up" (John 2:19). He said on another occasion: "For as Jonas was three days and three nights in the whale's belly; so shall the Son of man be three days and three nights in the heart of the earth" (Matt. 12:40). The crucifixion on Wednesday thus fulfills this prophecy. However, in addition to this fixing of the time of the Last Supper, the beginning of the new Love Feast, we discover the remaining words of the verse to be of deep significance to us, for they set forth the very basis for His coming into the world.

A. In Spite of His Coming Death.

Jesus well knew that the next day His enemies would nail Him to the cross. He was fully conscious that His last hours on earth were at hand when it was appointed "that he should depart," the Greek expression for the act of going from one place, or sphere, to another. It is wonderful to note that nothing which Jesus could suffer would quench His love; and His method of departure was the uttermost test and proof of His love. "Jesus knew" and "He loved." Between these two phrases we discover what He knew, and how He loved His own, and made plans for them which would mean much to them later.

B. In Spite of Their Condition.

We need to remember that this little band included Peter who had made his boasts of love, but who in a short time would deny Him. It included Thomas who would declare his doubts aloud. It included Judas, who in a brief time would go out into the night to betray Him. It included the other disciples about whom it was later written—". . . Then all the disciples forsook him and fled" (Matt. 26:56)..

C. Unto the Uttermost.

He loved with a limitless love, with the greatest love known in the universe, and with a love without end. God's love never changes, never ceases—any more than the sun ceases to shine, although men may hide in caves and dungeons from its light. What a contrast to earthly love! Have you read the story of the writing of the hymn: "O Love That Wilt Not Let Me Go"? George Matheson was a great Scottish preacher. Upon the eve of his graduation, his doctor told him that he would soon become totally blind. That evening he went to the home of the lady to whom he was engaged and told her what the doctor had said. As they sat together he told her: "I have no right to hold you to your promise now. I love you, and always will, but you are free to make your own choice." For a long time they sat with their hands twined together, and finally she withdrew her hand, and walked away. He left her presence and went to his own room. Late that night he sat down and wrote the lines of that which has now become one of the great hymns of the church.

II. THE LORD WASHES HIS DISCIPLES' FEET (John 13:2-5)

A. Judas the Traitor (v. 2).

Earlier in Christ's ministry there had been strife between the disciples as to who should have the chief seats. Now, during this supper with His disciples (the NASB is more correct here as it reads, "during supper")

Jesus washed the feet of His disciples. But into the story is injected an important word for us concerning Judas, the betrayer. Satan had already put into the heart of Judas the thought of betrayal (v. 2). Let us remember that there was still hope for Judas, since he was not so utterly lost as to plan his treachery all by himself. Satan opened the door and Judas looked in at the riches. Satan was the sower of the seed, but Judas had, for a long time, been preparing the soil of his heart to receive the evil seed. Through anger at the reproof of Jesus for complaining of Mary's waste of ointment and through his love of money (cf. John 12:4-7 with Matt. 26:14-16) the suggestion of Satan may have come. The thing we need to see here is that Judas was willing to follow the suggestion of Satan. Not until a man yields and says yes to his suggestions can Satan gain control of him. Judas had a great desire for money. This was his weakness. He did not yield to Christ in his heart. Satan worked on his weakness. Gradually Judas gave in more and more to Satan's temptings until he finally succumbed. Satan found Judas ready for the foul betrayal of Jesus and caused the plan to form in his mind. After this it was but one short step until Satan actually entered into Judas and possessed him (John 13:26-27). The end came quickly when Satan was through with Judas, and he committed suicide (Matt. 27:3-5). This is the perfect illustration of James 1:14-15.

B. Jesus Washes the Disciples' Feet (vv. 4-5).

Here again is additional evidence that this could not have been the Passover, for the Passover meal was to be eaten while standing. For this meal, they had reclined as was the custom, and now Jesus arose and laid aside His garments. After that He girded a towel around himself and poured water into a basin. He then began to wash the feet of the disciples one by one, drying them with the towel. Two great truths are portrayed in this simple act of our Lord. He laid aside His garments. This is the perfect illustration, the graphic picture of the incarnation. He had laid aside the garments of glory some thirty-three years before this time, and stepped down to take the form of a man. The Apostle Paul describes it beautifully for us in Philippians 2:5-8. Then came the actual washing of the feet of the disciples when Jesus poured the water into a basin, and began to wash their feet. The illustration He presented was that of His future work. He not only came into the world to die for sinners, but He also arose again, and lives today to do His work of daily cleansing and sanctifying of our lives.

III. THE MEANING OF THE WASHING (John 13:6-11)

As Jesus was washing the feet of the disciples, He came to the Apostle Peter and we are told that Peter was astounded, "dost thou wash my feet?" The disciples did not understand what was going on. If this had been simply the ceremony of physical cleansing so often talked about, then why would the disciples have even questioned His washing their feet? Without doubt, these people did have a custom of providing a basin for the washing of their guests' feet as they came into the house. But Jesus was not performing an ordinary act of washing their feet, for they had already been at the table, and in the midst of the supper Jesus arose to wash their feet. Because of this action, Peter was confounded.

Our Lord's answer to Peter clearly proves that He intended this act to convey some great spiritual teaching which they would understand later. "What I do thou knowest not now; but thou shalt know hereafter" (v. 7). If it had been the ordinary, everyday washing, it would not have required special explanation. This was something new. Moreover, if the disciples had had the customary washing in mind, all that Jesus said as He proceeded would only have added to the confusion.

Peter, still unsatisfied, now refused to allow Jesus to wash his feet (v. 8). As a matter of fact, he used the strongest language possible when he put it into the negative: "Thou shalt by no means wash my feet as long as the world stands" seems to be an excellent rendering of the words, "Thou shall never wash my feet." Chrysostom says: "No, not with hands that opened eyes, and cleansed lepers, and raised the dead." Peter had not yet learned his lesson. He was still the impulsive servant of the Lord. How often he boasted of his faithfulness only to be shown how shallow were his words. He did not understand, therefore, he would not permit the Lord to do this to him.

A. The Necessity of the Washing (v. 8).

And now we come to the key for the entire passage, for after this strong refusal, Jesus replied: "If I wash thee not you will have no fellowship with me" (Norlie Translation). That the word "part" means "fellowship" can easily be seen by reading other verses where the same word is used in the original. An excellent illustration is that of II Corinthians 6:15 which reads: "And what concord hath Christ with Belial? or what part [fellowship] hath he that believeth with an infidel?" Why was this true? Because the first condition of fellowship with Christ is submission to

Christ, even though the believer cannot understand all the reasons for the command. Then too, because this washing was symbolical of a spiritual cleansing, and Peter himself now understood (v. 9). If he were not cleansed from his pride and selfishness, he could not belong to a kingdom whose very heart is that of love. He must have the spirit of Christ before he can do the work of Christ.

We need to be very careful that we see it was not the physical washing which was essential, but the spiritual truth which it was meant to portray. No man is saved from his sin by baptism in water, but the spiritual truth which the act of baptism portrays is essential. So too, continued fellowship with Christ is dependent upon having our lives cleansed from sins by the living Christ (I John 1:6-9). This was the spiritual meaning of the washing which Peter would later understand; that Christ not only died for our sins, but that He also lives to keep us saved (cf. Rom. 5:10). If we never sinned, we would not need to have our feet washed. But because we do sin, we need that daily cleansing from sin of which feet washing is such a picturesque symbol.

Baptism symbolizes the justification of the sinner at the time of his salvation. This is a once-for-all justification, and, therefore, the rite of baptism should take place shortly after conversion. The Christian life begins at the time of the new birth, and it is here that Christ makes provision for us to live as Christians. At the new birth it was salvation from the penalty of sin. Now it is salvation from the power of sin as we live for Christ in this world of sin. His present work is that of setting us apart from the practice of sin, which is present tense salvation. Of this work of cleansing and daily sanctification, the washing of the saints' feet is the symbol, just as baptism in water is the symbol of justification. Dr. Bernard Schneider tells the story of a mother who had told her son, Freddy, to fill the woodbox. Freddy replied that he already had filled it, which was not quite the truth. Later on that night, mother knelt with Freddy at his bedside for their usual evening prayer. After mother had prayed there was a long silence, and she wondered why Freddy did not pray. Suddenly, he got up to his feet saying, "Guess I'd better take a look at that woodbox once more." His heart told him that he could not pray with that lie there. He went out to fill the woodbox and then came back to pray.

Even so, we cannot pray nor have sweet fellowship with the Lord while there is unconfessed sin in our hearts. We need to daily confess our sins to Him. When we confess: "He is faithful and just to forgive us our sins, and to cleanse us from all unrighteousness" (I John 1:9). This is His present work as He sits at the right hand of the Father, interceding in our behalf. For this wonderful present work, He has given us the visual demonstration as a symbol, the washing of the saints' feet.

B. The Misunderstanding of Peter (v. 9).

Once again we see the impetuousness of Peter. He was constantly moving on the impulse of the moment. The Lord had suggested that Peter's failure to have his feet washed would impair fellowship; hence, since fellowship is in question, he wants to get all he can, and asks for more than his feet. He wants to be washed—including his hands and his head.

C. The Explanation of Jesus (v. 10).

Jesus immediately portrays the complete picture as He answers Peter. Actually, a bit of word study is important here, for Jesus used two different words in His answer. The first word "washed" is bathed in the original, and an entirely different word is used for the word translated "washed" a little later in the verse. So the verse could well be translated to read: "He that is bathed needeth not save to wash his feet, for he is clean all over." When a person takes a bath, he does not have to wash all over again except as his feet have become soiled in the dust of the streets as he walked from the bathhouse. (Remember, they used public bathhouses in the day of our Lord.) The spiritual truth is very plain. When a person is saved, he is saved once and for all eternity, and does not have to be saved over again once a quarter, or once a year, or each time he breaks fellowship with the Lord through sin. This does not mean that the Christian deliberately walks out into the world with intent to sin. It does not give license to sin. It does mean that the Christian is still walking in a sinful world, and he does need daily cleansing. He needs sanctification. Let every believer keep these two separate. The sinner needs to be saved, and through it he is made a saint. The saint needs to be cleansed, and the washing of the saints' feet is the picture of that cleansing.

IV. THE OBSERVANCE OF THE RITE TODAY (John 13:12-17)

The Brethren Church practices the rite of Feet Washing as a part of the service of communion. Many churches do not observe this rite, and of course this raises questions concerning the rite. Should Christians observe the washing of the feet as a part of the observance of communion which is an ordinance of the church? A very simple reading of the English text will answer the question for us. There are three words used by our Lord which compel us to believe that it is for Christians now, even as it was for them in the night in which Jesus began the rite.

A. "Ought" (v. 14).

This is a strong word that carries with it the implication of moral obligation, meaning it is the only right thing to do in the matter. It is like saying that a Christian ought to read the Bible, or ought to pray, or ought to pay his debts. The very context adds weight to the argument, for He said: "Ye call me Master and Lord: and ye say well; for so I am. If I then, your Lord and Master, have washed your feet; ye also ought to wash one another's feet" (vv. 13-14). As Master and Lord, He is the supreme authority. Actually, this simply means that He is the superintendent or supervisor of my life, and, as such, He has the right to tell me what to do. He not only tells us what to do, but was willing to demonstrate, and thus became the first to wash the feet of His followers. How anyone can miss the meaning of this word "ought" is beyond comprehension. To deliberately avoid the meaning is to disobey.

B. "Example" (v. 15).

Again and again in the New Testament, we read the word "example." God reminds us that the things which happened to the Israelites in their journey through the wilderness "were our examples" (I Cor. 10), and were permitted to come to them to remind us to avoid the pitfalls. So here, He gives us an example in a positive direction. We are to do as He has shown us. An example which we are to follow is meant to be imitated, or lived up to, in the most minute detail. So often men look to examples which are imperfect, and, in short order, the copy becomes imperfect. Not so, with the example which Christ gave us. He, the perfect example, did all things perfectly so that men were compelled to say they could find no fault in Him.

C. "Do" (v. 17).

The third word which emphasizes the importance of the observance of this rite is found in the fact that in the doing of it, Jesus promised blessing. This is one of the conditional promises of the Bible. Some of God's promises are unconditional. They are facts regardless of the direction we may take. He promised that "My grace is sufficient . . ." (II Cor. 12:9), and it is sufficient for every testing and trial. This is unconditional. But with the promise of this verse, the condition is: "If ye know these things, happy are ye if ye do them." The obedience to this command has brought untold blessings to many who have shared in the service of the washing of the saints' feet. How often we have listened to the testimony of the joy that has come to the hearts of both older and younger Christians as they have participated in the communion service.

Once on a recent occasion, I came through the coal mining section of our country and saw a picture at which I never cease to marvel. The miners where just changing shifts, and I saw dozens of them as they emerged from the darkness of the mine to the light of the day. Their hands, faces, and clothing were grimy and black, but everyone of them had a brilliance of the eye that was unbelievable. Those who know about it tell us that the eyes of the miner are clear and lustrous because the fountain of tears in the lachrymal gland is ever pouring its gentle tides over the eye, cleansing away each speck of dust as soon as it alights. This is the miracle of cleansing which our lives need momentarily in such a world as this. And this is what our blessed Lord is prepared to do for us if we will come to Him for cleansing. This is what the service of Feet Washing portrays—the daily and momentary cleansing by our wonderful Saviour.

In giving this symbol to the church, the Lord Jesus gave a visual demonstration of two great truths in relation to the matter of Christian life and the holiness of that life. Because He gave us the symbol of the washing of the feet, He showed the error of claiming such complete and absolute goodness for the Christian to be incapable of committing sin. But over against it is the other extreme which declares that man is so weak in the flesh that in spite of the indwelling of the Holy Spirit he is obliged to continue in willful sinning.

Christ is the perfect example for every Christian as to his walk. The symbol of Feet Washing recognizes the human weakness, and, therefore, the need of repeated cleansing. The cleansing which He gives points to the fact that He is able to keep us from falling, and the Feet Washing service should point us to the only power the Christian has for a life of holiness. Paul picks it up in Ephesians 5:26 when he reminds us of this sanctifying and cleansing with "the washing of water by the word."

There is one word of caution that should be spoken. The rite of Feet Washing, even as a part of the communion service, like every other rite the Lord has given, may be perverted now as it was in the early days of the church. It may be kept in the letter of the observance only, and not in the spirit. It may be observed without the discerning, that is, the cleansing of the heart, or the spirit of humble and loving service. It may bring condemnation instead of blessing. But all of this does not detract from the total value of the ordinance when it is rightly observed.

The Lord's Supper

****

CHAPTER SEVEN

THE CHAPTER OUTLINED:

I. Biblical Background
 A. The Lord's Supper
 B. The Love Feast
 C. Not the Passover

II. The Spiritual Significance
 A. A Memorial Service
 B. A Symbol
 C. A Type

III. The Observance
 A. Correction of Abuse
 B. Continue the Observance
 C. Manner of Observance
 D. Preparation for the Observance

SUGGESTED BACKGROUND DEVOTIONAL READING

Monday—The Supper Instituted (Matt. 26:17-30)

Tuesday—A Large Upper Room (Mark 14:12-26)

Wednesday—Gathered at the Table (Luke 22:7-21)

Thursday—Before the Feast of Passover (John 13:1-5)

Friday—Lord's Supper and Abuse (I Cor. 11:20-34)

Saturday—Love One Another (I John 3:10-24)

Sunday—Herein Is Love (I John 4:7-21)

The communion service is another beautiful memorial given to the church by the Lord. A careful study of the institution of this service will convince the student of God's Word that a threefold service involving the Washing of the Feet, the Lord's Supper, and the Communion of The Bread and the Cup, gives us the picture Christ intended.

It is very common in our own generation, and those gone before, to celebrate victories in the lives of the people whom we desire to honor by serving a banquet. It may be an athletic banquet, a marriage feast, a political one-hundred-dollar-a-plate dinner, a victory banquet for a successful charity drive, or some other matter that deserves a celebration. So too, the Lord's Supper is a celebration of a victory that has been won, but the final celebration will not come until the Marriage Supper of the Lamb. Each time we observe the Lord's Supper we have the privilege of a foretaste of that great supper.

I. BIBLICAL BACKGROUND (John 13:2, 4; I Cor. 11:20; Luke 22:20)

There are two general terms applied to this feast or supper, namely; the *Lord's Supper,* and the *Love Feast.* Each of these names has special significance and comes to us from the Word of God.

A. The Lord's Supper.

The Lord's Supper, a name most commonly given to this service, gains its name from the very fact that it was instituted by the Lord Jesus himself in the upper room on the night before His trial and crucifixion. In the institution of the service, John records, "And supper being ended," or actually, *during supper* (John 13:2). When the Apostle Paul writes concerning the matter he says, "When ye come together therefore into one place, this is not to eat the Lord's supper" (I Cor. 11:20). Two important truths are here. It was "the *Lord's* supper" (unique), and this because He instituted it with certain memorial values in view; and, likewise, because it looked forward to the Marriage Supper of the Lamb of God, even Jesus Christ the Saviour. It was a *supper.* The word used here always refers to a meal, and William Smith in his *Dictionary of Antiquity* describes it as "the principal meal of the day." It was usually eaten rather late in the day and frequently not before sunset.

That it is not simply the eating of a bite of bread or the sipping of the fruit of the vine is very evident not only from the institution of the service in which definite reference is made to supper, but also in the words of Paul as he attempted to correct the error that had crept into the serving of the meal.

B. The Love Feast.

The Love Feast describes the essential characteristics of the meal; namely, it is a feast of love among those who love one another. Chapter 13 of John begins with the statement of Christ's love for His own, and concludes with what He himself calls a new commandment: "That ye love one another; as I have loved you, that ye also love one another" (cf. John 13:1, 34-35). The Apostle Jude uses the term in reference to the meal as if it were a term familiar to all of his readers (Jude 1:12). The entire thought of this holy love is taught only in the Bible. Classical Greek has no comparable word. C. F. Yoder in his book *God's Means of Grace* says: "The Love Feast which the Lord instituted was so different from the social feasts of that day that a new name had to be coined to distinguish it from the feasts of that day, and it is so different from the feasts of popular churches today, that the name should be preserved. It is not the abbreviated form or sacrament of the Eucharist, wrongly called The Lord's Supper by many churches. . . . It is a sacred meal because it represents and pictures the sacred love of God in the hearts of His people."

C. Not the Passover.

A further detail of Biblical background is essential; namely, that the Lord's Supper, or the Love Feast is not a continuation, or an observance of the Passover. The chronology of the institution of what is now generally referred to as the communion service is of vital importance in the interpretation of many related passages of Scripture. The statement of each of the writers of the four Gospels places the meal which Jesus ate, and which is the foundation upon which the Lord's Supper is based, one day prior to the Passover Feast. The preparation day is clearly marked as the day on which the meal took place. The disciples recognized the Passover as future, for when Judas went out from the supper, "some of them thought, because Judas had the bag, that Jesus had said unto him, Buy those things that we have need against the feast . . ." (John 13:29). Jesus had declared, while at the supper, that He would not eat this Passover with them (Luke 22:16). He could not eat of the Passover, for He was to be our Passover Lamb. Paul reminds us ". . . For even Christ our passover is sacrificed for us: Therefore let us keep the feast, not with old leaven, neither with the leaven of malice and wickedness . . ." (I Cor. 5:7-8).

There are many other details that teach us specifically that it could not have been the Passover as it was not called a supper, but a feast. This meal is referred to as "supper." As study is given to the Passover, there are many laws which the disciples violated if this had been the Passover: (a) the penalty of death was inflicted on those who ate early (Num. 9:10-13); (b) no one was to leave the house until morning, but the disciples all left the upper room before midnight (Exod. 12:22). The Passover was to be eaten with shoes on and the participants standing (Exod. 12:11), but at this supper, they did not have on their shoes, and they reclined. Hence, this is something brand new, not only in the breaking of the bread, and taking of the cup, but actually in the meal itself, which has now been made the Love Feast.

II. THE SPIRITUAL SIGNIFICANCE

What is there about this celebration which makes it significantly different from any other meal that might be eaten by the same group of people gathered together? We need to be reminded at frequent intervals that the first Lord's Supper was held at a strategic point in the life and ministry of our Lord. He was on His way to the cross to become our Passover, and in the midst of it, He paused to celebrate this service—the first communion service with His disciples. The Bible clearly declares that at this moment "his hour was come . . ." (John 13:1) and that ". . . the Father had given all things into his hands . . ." (John 13:3). This covers the entire service of the communion, not only the Washing of the Feet, and the Eucharist, but also the ordinance of the Lord's Supper. The apostles carried it on regularly after the death of Christ, which is evidenced in numerous Scriptures (I Cor. 5:7; 11:17-34; II Peter 2:13; Jude 12).

The supper was in very essence a spiritual observance, for the Apostle Paul tells us (I Cor. 11:34) that it was not for the purpose of satisfying hunger, leaving only a single purpose of picturing truth. The table was to be kept free from divisions among the people (I Cor. 11:18-19); it was to be free from over-indulgence of food (I Cor. 11:21-22), and all selfishness was to be cleared away (I Cor. 11:33).

Since this is not an ordinary meal, eaten in an ordinary manner, what then is the real meaning of the Love Feast?

A. A Memorial Service.

It is a part of the memorial service of communion and is to constantly remind us of the love of Christ. As pointed out earlier, the introduction to the entire service in John 13 makes special reference to the love of Christ in behalf of His own. A common problem among all mankind is that of forgetfulness. We take so many things for granted that unless they are frequently called to mind, good as they may be, we forget them. We need this memorial to remind us of the love of God which was manifested in the Lord Jesus.

There is nothing greater in all the world than His love for us. And when as believers we come together to celebrate His feast, it is a memorial to His love, and the very center of our thoughts should be upon Christ. This helps us to understand why Peter and Jude both denounce those hypocrites who by their own revelings spoiled the significance of the feast.

Selfishness was contrary to the love which Jesus demonstrated at the institution of this feast, and it is as inappropriate today as it was on the night of the institution. As a further illustration of the depths of that love, a rereading of the chapter will remind us of the love with which Jesus in a final gesture offered himself to Judas. The world has never known a love greater than that of Jesus in which a man laid down his life for his enemies. The Love Feast, which commemorates that love, ought to be a glorious feast of remembrance, and for this very reason should attract every believer.

B. A Symbol.

The Love Feast is also a symbol. It was during this supper that Jesus gave His disciples a "new commandment"; namely, that they should have the same love one for the other that He had for them. Just in the manner in which the feast reminds us of the love of Christ for us, it becomes the symbol of the love which we should show one to another. He went so far as to suggest that this kind of love is one of the badges of discipleship. "By this shall all men know that ye are my disciples, if ye have love one to another" (John 13:35). And before the evening was over, He prayed, ". . . the love wherewith thou hast loved me may be in them, and I in them" (John 17:26). So, in three distinct ways Jesus gave to us the truth of loving one another by example, by commandment, and by prayer. No wonder the apostles were so anxious to meet together for the Love Feast. It can only cause us to ask: "Why do Christians today absent themselves from the table of the Lord?"

Eating together has always been an act of friendliness and love. We find it in Old Testament days in the illustrations of Melchizedek and Abraham (Gen. 14:17-18), and of the many religious feasts of the Jews as outlined in the feasts of Passover, First Fruits, and various offerings. One of the accusations brought against Jesus was found in the fact that He ate and drank with publicans and sinners.

C. A Type.

The Love Feast is a picture of what is to come, and, frequently, the Lord has given us pictures that represent, at least in part, that which is to come. For example, when the Lord walked upon the earth, He frequently used the picture of a feast to represent His kingdom. He did this in the Parable of the Marriage Feast (Matt. 21:1-13); the Parable of the Great Supper (Luke 15:16ff).

But specifically as He came to the institution of the Last Supper, He said to His disciples: "But I say unto you, I will not drink henceforth of this fruit of the vine, until that day when I drink it new with you in my Father's kingdom" (Matt. 26:29). He had been supping with them in fellowship and love, but then declared that He would not do it again until the Kingdom age. However, the very meal which was inaugurated on that night became the picture of a future day. We find the fulfillment of it described fully in Revelation 19:7-9.

The Apostle Paul reminds us in Ephesians 1:3 that when we become believers we are ". . . blessed . . . with all spiritual blessings in heavenly places in Christ," but this is only a foretaste of what it shall be. Paul describes it: "Which is the earnest of our inheritance until the redemption of the purchased possession, unto the praise of his glory" (Eph. 1:14).

The Love Feast is a type which points to the time when this foretaste of heavenly fellowship shall give way to the fullness of the heavenly life. All the earthly gifts and possessions shall pass away. Faith shall become sight, hope shall become fruition, and love—the eternal, abiding love of God—shall be an eternal feast. It is this love that shines through the Love Feast as a memorial, a symbol, and a type.

III. THE OBSERVANCE (I Cor. 11:17-34)

Paul wrote to the Corinthian church concerning the observance of this feast, warning of certain problems that had crept into the observance of the feast. Because of this warning, some have come to the conclusion that the Love Feast should be eliminated. However, even a simple reading of this passage will show the fallacy of this position.

A. Correction of Abuse.

Note in the passage, there is not one word of discouragement against the feast itself, but rather a simple attempt to correct the disorders that had arisen in the observance of it. To correct the abuse of a thing is not to remove the object itself. The difficulty was simply that there were factions among them, and they were literally attempting to outdo each other in the matter of the supper itself.

B. Continue the Observance.

The Apostle here talks about the supper in a very familiar manner, which indicates that the Corinthian Christians had been regularly partaking of the supper following the direction given in its institution. The latter verses of the chapter actually give direction, that when ". . . ye come together to eat, wait for one another," indicating that even though it is not a direct command, at least its implication is that the church should continue the observance of the supper.

C. Manner of Observance.

Perhaps the most important truth of the entire passage, as far as the supper is concerned, is that the church is urged to observe the supper not for the gratification of the physical appetite, but rather for the spiritual truth which it portrays. "If any man hunger, let him eat at home . . ." (v. 34). The Love Feast is not to satisfy hunger, but to share together real Christian fellowship both one with another and with the Lord Jesus in whose name we meet. This in itself should give some direction as to the manner of observance, in which those gathered together should converse primarily about the things of the Lord, His blessings toward us, and the joy we have in fellowship with Him and one another. Too often, now that the food has become a minor matter, the conversation has become the primary concern, and unfortunately the conversation is not concerning things of the Lord.

D. Preparation for the Observance.

While it is true that the service of Feet Washing should prepare the hearts of believers for the entire communion service, it is likewise true that the Love Feast should be a special preparation for the partaking of The Bread and the Cup. Sitting down to the table of the Lord should speak to all men everywhere of the unity of the body of Christ in a very special way. The tragedy which Paul saw in this Corinthian church was in the fact that there were some divisions among them. To come to the table of the Lord with divisions and strifes or alienations is nothing short of sin. Believers are to sit as brethren. Before we eat together, every wrong shall be righted, and every grievance healed.

This section of Paul's letter (I Cor. 11:17-22) also reminds us in a very practical manner of the truth that the very things which the Lord has given to man for his blessing, may become in reality a curse in misuse. The institution of this service was given the night in which Christ was betrayed. It is still possible for Christians, even in the observance of the Lord's Supper, to betray Him through misuse, and turn that which is intended for blessing into curse.

It is the Lord's Supper, therefore, there is no place for arrogance and conceit. When we come to His table, we ought not to think on ourselves, our excellencies, our accomplishments, but rather on Him, who through His death and resurrection rescued us from the dominion of sin. To choose a special place at the table in order to avoid being seated beside one that we may not think is in our same class, would be to look at self instead of Christ. It is the Lord's Supper, therefore, it should be reserved for the Lord's people, and they should come to the table without thought of position in life, except that of being in the family of God through Christ.

It is the Lord's Supper, therefore, there is no room for division. Christ calls men to His table as followers of the Lord, and this is to one body. We are members of that body. We once knew two women who partook regularly of the Lord's Supper and even sat at the same table, but who had not spoken to one another as neighbors for more than twenty years. The battle had waged between them over a very insignificant event that happened in a club to which both women had belonged. The division came into the church and although often seated near one another, they did not speak. Paul reminds us in this passage that to cherish a spirit of division is to run counter to the command of Christ to "love one another." Why obey one of Christ's commands and deliberately choose to disobey another?

It is the Lord's Supper, therefore, there is no room for gluttony. Some of the Corinthians apparently loved their food more than they did their brethren. They ate greedily, not even waiting the coming of the other brethren. By their own physical appetites, they detracted from a spiritual meal the very spiritual atmosphere that should have made the feast one of joy and fellowship.

CONCLUSION

In summing up all of this, we turn to several things which have been written by others on this very wonderful truth of God's Word, concerning this part of the communion service.

Dr. C. F. Yoder in writing concerning the Love Feast says: "The practical benefits resulting from the observance of the Love Feast is proof of the divine wisdom in establishing it." In the apostolic church it was at the Love Feast that the rich and poor were brought together in equality (Acts 2:43-47). The churches which properly observe the Love Feast are characterized by a larger sense of brotherhood than is found in those that have discarded it. To satisfy a longing for fellowship, they often have turned to other kinds of social affairs and clubs, which seek to satisfy the flesh rather than minister to the spirit, and which work evil to the church rather than good.

In speaking of the Love Feast, Minucius Felix, a second century church father, said: "We share in our banquets which are not only modest, but also sober . . . Thus we love one another, to your regret, with a mutual love because we do not know how to hate. Thus we call one another brethren as being men born of one God, and companions in faith, and fellow heirs in hope."

Add to that, the statement of Clement of Alexandria, as he wrote concerning the Love Feast. "The supper is made for love, but the supper is not love; only a proof of reciprocal kindly feeling."

The Bread and the Cup

****

CHAPTER EIGHT

THE CHAPTER OUTLINED:

I. The Institution of the Ordinance
   A. Transubstantiation
   B. Consubstantiation
   C. Symbolical — Memorial

II. The Purpose of the Ordinance
   A. It is a Memorial
   B. It is a Proclamation
   C. It Is a New Covenant
   D. It Is a Promise

III. Preparation for Observing the Ordinance
   A. Thoughtlessness
   B. Ignorance
   C. Unconfessed Sin

SUGGESTED BACKGROUND DEVOTIONAL READING

Monday—The Bread and the Cup (Matt. 26:26-30)

Tuesday—"My Body . . . My Blood" (Mark 14:22-26)

Wednesday—Until the Kingdom Comes (Luke 22:14-20)

Thursday—"In Remembrance of Me" (I Cor. 11:23-28)

Friday—The Old Covenant (Exod. 24:1-8)

Saturday—The Old a Figure of the New (Heb. 9:1-10)

Sunday—The New Covenant (Heb. 9:11-28)

There are many ways in which memorials have been established to help keep alive the achievements of men and women. Our nation's capital is filled with beautiful memorials of various sizes and shapes. There is the tall Washington Monument which stands like a guardian over the city. There is the beautiful Lincoln Memorial, with the statue of Abraham Lincoln to remind men of his leadership in an hour of grave crisis. Then in Gettysburg there is the cemetery filled with statues and tombstones commemorating the terrible battle of the Civil War and the cost of freedom. Some famous persons have public buildings and churches named after them as a reminder of their worthwhile contributions to mankind.

Perhaps the most famous of present-day mausoleums is that of the Taj Mahal, near Agra, India. This was built by the emperor Shah Jehan for himself and his wife, Mumtaz Mahal, who died in 1629. It is said that twenty thousand men worked on it for twenty-two years. It is 190 feet high and 130 feet long and made of white marble.

But in this study in the series on the ordinance of the communion service, we discover the memorial which Jesus established for himself among His followers. A tomb could not be built for His memorial, for He could not be bound to a tomb. Then, too, a material tomb would eventually crumble and in the course of centuries be completely forgotten by men. Then without doubt, Jesus knew how few would be able to make the long trip to Palestine to see any kind of a memorial if it were erected. In addition, He was anxious that men should neither worship, nor cherish a shrine. Hence, He instituted the communion service—a threefold memorial service consisting of The Love Feast, Feet Washing, and the communion of The Bread and the Cup.

I. THE INSTITUTION OF THE ORDINANCE (Luke 24:14-20; I Cor. 11:23-28)

During the supper hour, Tuesday evening preceding the Passover, the Lord instituted the communion of The Bread and the Cup, now commonly referred to as the Eucharist. He used unleavened bread, for remember, during the entire week preceding the Passover, there was to be no leaven in the house. Jesus took the bread, and did just as He had done when He fed the five thousand and the four thousand—breaking, blessing, and distributing it to the disciples. This was so much the custom of Christ that after the Resurrection He was known thereby (Luke 24:30-31). The act of blessing, sanctifies and makes sacred that which is thus received. By this act, He manifested His thankfulness to God, and set the article apart as a suitable and becoming emblem—common, unleavened bread. Likewise the cup—the fruit of the vine. A very simple reading of the institution of this part of the ordinance will help us in the interpretation of it. Luke 22:19-20 tells us what He did: "He took bread, and gave thanks, and brake it, and gave unto them . . . Likewise also the cup after supper . . . ." Then the same passage indicates that He explained it by saying: "This is my body which is given for you: this do in remembrance of me." And concerning the cup, He said: "This cup is the new testament in my blood, which is shed for you."

Three interpretations of the meaning of The Bread and the Cup have been adopted by various groups, and we simply look at them now.

A. Transubstantiation.

The Roman Catholic Church teaches that at the words of consecration during the mass, the emblems cease to be bread and wine and become the actual body and blood of Christ. When Christ instituted the service, however, He said: "This is my body . . . this is the new testament in my blood . . . ." Yet He was still standing before them alive and had not gone to the cross. The emblems, therefore, must be symbolical in their meaning. The teaching that Christ suffers anew every time the mass is observed, is, of course, unscriptural: "For Christ is not entered into the holy place made with hands. . . . Nor yet that he could offer himself often . . . ; For then must he often have suffered since the foundation of the world: but now once in the end of the world . . . Christ was once offered to bear the sins of many . . ." (Heb. 9:24-28).

B. Consubstantiation.

This is the teaching that while the bread and wine continue to be bread and wine, they are actually joined with the body and blood of Christ at the moment they enter the body of the person partaking of the emblems. This view is held by many Lutheran bodies, and those who follow their theological pattern.

C. Symbolical—Memorial.

The third view which is held by most Protestant churches today, and which is the New Testament teaching, is that the emblems are symbols representing His body and His blood. This is the position first advocated by Zwingli after the break with Rome. Christ did not say: "This do in sacrifice of me," nor "This do for the pardon of sins, for the living or for the dead." But He did say, ". . . this do in remembrance of me."

II. THE PURPOSE OF THE ORDINANCE

We are not left in the dark as to why Christ instituted the ordinance of the communion service. He very clearly suggests several purposes in its very institution.

A. It Is a Memorial (Luke 22:19; I Cor. 11:24-25).

Both Luke and the Apostle Paul, writing under the direction of the Holy Spirit, are careful to suggest that the Lord Jesus established the ordinance in "remembrance of me." Regularly we hear about Jesus and His work in our behalf as we study in our Sunday Schools, or read in our Bibles, or listen as the pastor ministers the Word. But in a peculiar manner when we gather to break bread and drink the cup, we are brought by way of a visual aid to see a bit of the meaning of His death and to recall it anew.

The very emblems that were chosen by the Lord are fitting emblems. The bread is a whole parable of suffering love. First the seed was planted and had to die before it could spring into life and become living grain. Then the grain had to be beaten and crushed before it could become flour for the making of bread. The meal had to be kneaded and exposed to intense heat in the fiery oven before it could become bread. All of this is the picture of Christ who declared himself to be the "bread of life."

Then the cup. The wine is crushed from the grape and flows like the living blood telling of life poured out. Could there be a more perfect picture of the Saviour's very life given for and to us? We are to partake of The Bread and the Cup in order to bring back to our minds that which we are so prone to forget: *His death in our stead.* Someone has said that we remember 10 percent of what we hear, 80 percent of what we see, and 90 percent of what we do. Here is a memorial in which we *hear* His Word, as it is read, we *see* the emblems as they are upon the table, and we *do* as we partake of The Bread and the Cup.

When we come to the table of the Lord and finally to the Eucharist, breaking the bread and drinking the cup of communion, we honor our blessed Lord, and indeed actually thank Him for His death in our behalf. No wonder He instituted it! No wonder this moment has become a very sacred moment for God's people. It is here that His presence seems more evident, His touch more real. With the symbols—The Bread and the Cup—upon our lips, we somehow know more of His love, and are able to say with the songwriter: "If ever I loved Thee, my Jesus, 'tis now." Just as bread strengthens us, so this bit of bread pictures new strength for our spiritual lives. And just as the cup brings refreshment to our bodies, so this cup symbolizes the spiritual refreshment that is in Christ Jesus our Lord.

B. It Is a Proclamation (I Cor. 11:26).

The words "ye do shew" means to proclaim, or to declare. The message is very clear "... ye do shew the Lord's death...." The Lord did not ask His followers to remember His life, His miracles, His good works (although all of these are important and wonderful), but rather He selected from among all the moments of His life on earth that very moment when He hung upon the cross, and cried: "... My God, my God, why hast thou forsaken me?" (Mark 15:34). He wants us to remember His death, and asks us to show it forth. It was to die that He came into the world, and He wants us to continue to tell men through this picture about that death.

There is a very special sense in which when we partake of The Bread and the Cup, we are proclaiming our part in the death of Christ. We are saying in essence: "It was my sin that broke His body, and my sin that caused Him to shed His blood." A sermon or a lesson tells of His death through words. The Bread and the Cup are a symbol of His death.

The tragedy of the entire service is that so many partake of it in such a superficial manner, either as a mere form and something that makes it appear that they are religious, or as a sacrament through which they gain merit and favor with God. As believers we should help one another to see that this is a wonderful privilege not to be entered into lightly, nor neglected because of sin in our lives, but an opportunity to "shew forth His death."

C. It Is a New Covenant (Matt. 26:28; Luke 22:20; I Cor. 11:25).

The "new testament" to which Jesus referred is the same as a covenant in the Old Testament. It actually is a contract or agreement between God and His people. Jesus suggests that it is a "new testament" or contract. There was an old covenant or agreement between God and Israel which was given on Mount Sinai (cf. Exod. 19:5-8). This covenant was sealed for the people a short time afterwards by a solemn act in which the blood of the sacrifice was sprinkled, half of it on the altar, and the rest on the people after they had accepted the conditions of the agreement (cf. Exod. 24:7-8).

The new covenant which Christ brought is the new and better agreement by which all who believe in Christ are saved from all sin forever. This new covenant Christ sealed with His own blood. The condition of the old covenant was: "If ye will obey my voice indeed, and keep my covenant, then . . . ." It was another way of saying: "This do and live." The new covenant is different in that it said: *"Believe in Christ and live."* This is the covenant of grace, and is in sharp contrast to the covenant of the law in every aspect. This new covenant is made possible only because of the substitutionary death of Christ. His shed blood is the only seal for the covenant, and it is as sure as the blood itself. The blood of Jesus Christ is God's pledge that He will save all who believe. The blood of Christ seals to the world God's covenant of His grace.

To picture this covenant, He gave us The Bread and the Cup—the Eucharist—of the threefold communion service as an outward symbol of His agreement to save all who believe.

There hangs in many homes and offices, copies of the Constitution of the United States. Affixed to these copies is the copy of the seal of the United States Government. It is not the real thing, but represents the original copy with the seal fixed upon that original copy of the document, which is safely guarded in official quarters. So it is with the bread which we break, and the cup which we drink. It is not in any way to be construed as the real body and blood of Christ, but rather as a symbol of the real thing, which was given for us. It is, however, the visible evidence of the new agreement into which God has entered, and stands for the seal which has been affixed to the contract.

D. It Is a Promise (I Cor. 11:26; Matt. 26:29).

The words of the Apostle Paul, "till he come," record in very definite fashion the promise of the Lord Jesus that He is coming back to rule and reign upon the earth. Mark and Luke, as well as the statement recorded in Matthew, "until that day when I drink it new with you in my Father's kingdom," give to us His own promise or prophecy which through the years has been called the *Blessed Hope* of the church. When the Lord Jesus sat at the evening meal, and drank of the fruit of the vine, He was not defeated. He knew that this was His hour of greatest triumph, and that looking beyond the next three days in which He must suffer, die, and be buried—there would come the resurrection, and the ascension to His Father. He did not stop here, but went beyond to that moment when ". . . I will come again, and receive you unto myself . . ." (John 14:3).

It is true that by The Bread and the Cup we remember the death of Christ. But in that very death there is hope for the new day when Jesus shall come to receive us unto himself that where He is, we shall be also. Therefore, we "shew the Lord's death till he come." Then we will no longer observe the ordinance of the communion—the Washing of the Feet, the Lord's Supper (as a symbol), nor the Eucharist, for we shall be with Him. The results of His sacrificial death on the cross will be completed, and will be manifested to the whole world. Then ". . . we shall be like him; for we shall see him as he is." This simply means we shall have bodies in the resurrection like His resurrection body. What a glorious day that will be when all sin and sinning will be done away, even the very presence of sin. There will be no more sorrow, tears, pain, separation, loneliness, or death.

This ordinance is a picture of the new covenant. It will remain in force until Christ comes and renders it no longer essential for a memorial. The significance and force of the service should remain until that day.

III. PREPARATION FOR OBSERVING THE ORDINANCE

In this study, we have been involved in three chapters concerning the communion service as instituted by the Lord. It is a single institution, with three distinct parts—yet one service. They cannot be separated one from the other. The services of The Lord's Supper and of Feet Washing should be a preparation for the observance of The Bread and the Cup taken in remembrance of the Lord's death. But the Apostle, in writing to correct the errors of the Corinthian church, likewise, has left a warning for the church of today. Those errors (sins) involved arrogance, conceit, divisions among believers, gluttony, and even drunkenness. Now Paul adds this word, "let a man examine himself . . ." (I Cor. 11:28). This is the preparation we should make as we come to the communion table. We are not to come to examine or discover whether we are Christians. That should have been settled long before this hour; but rather to discover—and to know that we are in actual and habitual exercise of all that belongs to a true Christian life. We ought to come exercising our minds in recollection of His love for us, both in His life and His death. The communion service ought to bring us into a close communion with our wonderful Lord and send us out to serve Him in newness of the life which He gives.

The warning Paul gives us is that we are not to partake of The Bread and the Cup "unworthily." What is the meaning of the word? Many have absented themselves from the service declaring themselves to be unworthy, and, since the Bible declares they shall not eat because of this, they stay away. It certainly cannot mean our being worthy of Christ, nor of our being imperfect, for in that case none of us would qualify; nor could we, for none of us is worthy or perfect (cf. I Cor. 11:27-28). The word might better be translated "in an unworthy manner," and refers to the careless manner in which many come to partake of The Bread and the Cup. Paul describes for us that unworthy manner when in verse 29 he suggests "not discerning the Lord's body." Let us remember that the people in Corinth had become very careless in regard to the communion service, both in their attitude toward it, and in their manner of observing it. Some of the members were profaning this sacred ordinance by making it a common meal, and they ate and drank too much. Some even became intoxicated at the service, for they brought their own wine with them (I Cor. 11:20-21). This was not honoring the Lord in the communion of The Bread and the Cup, but a feast where they celebrated their own selfishness and pride and gave in to their own appetites. They actually were losing sight of the command of the Lord: "This do in remembrance of me." So we need to examine ourselves as individual Christians, to discover anything that hinders us from "discerning the Lord's body," which will cause us to eat and drink unworthily. The emblems are but mere symbols, but they must be eaten and drunk with reverence, thought and feeling. We must enter into the meaning of the service, and through the outward symbols enter into the spiritual meaning.

There are many things that may enter in to cause us to eat and drink in an unworthy manner.

A. Thoughtlessness.

We may come to the service without giving serious thought to the entire service. We may give ourselves solely to the things about us, and actually partake of The Bread and the Cup without ever giving one moment of thought to the death of Christ on the cross. We may do this in spite of the fact that the Word is read, the songs are sung, the prayers offered, and the elements given to us with proper instruction. This very lack of thought will lead to an irreverent participation in the entire service.

B. Ignorance.

Very often children are not aware of the true meaning of the service and come to the time of eating and drinking without sufficient knowledge. This frequently carries over to the adults. Prior to the service of communion, there should be very careful preparation on the part of pastors, teachers and parents to make sure that every individual has an understanding of the true meaning of the service. God does not condemn failure to understand, but He does hold those of us who have His truth responsible for giving it to those who share in the service.

C. Unconfessed Sin.

John reminds us in his first Epistle that: "If we confess our sins, he is faithful and just to forgive us our sins, and to cleanse us from all unrighteousness" (I John 1:9). As we study the Word, we discover that the Lord gave very explicit direction on every fundamental of the faith. He plainly stated the fact that all men are sinful and in desperate need of a Saviour. He assured the world that God is gracious and merciful, sending His own Son to be our Saviour. He declared that He is that Son of God, come into the world to give His life a ransom for men. He invited sinners to believe in Him, to turn to God for eternal life. He insisted that men must turn from sin and unbelief to faith and righteousness. He plainly warned of the doom of the wicked and unrepentant, and promised the glorious life to those who would receive Him as their personal Saviour. We cannot keep our sin and come to the table in a discerning manner, for Christ is the light of the world, and light has come into the world to dispel the darkness. We may be trying to do both, but this is making light of the work of Christ, and thus not discerning Him. If we hug sin, we cannot embrace the Saviour. Paul says: "For this cause many are weak and sickly . . . and many sleep" (I Cor. 11:30).

The remedy is to let a man examine himself, and then let him come to the communion. To examine ourselves is to do so in the light of all that we find in the Word of God. Let us remember that Christ is exalted on every page of the Book. To examine ourselves is to do so by God's Holy Spirit. He has come to convict and to reprove. As we permit Him to do His work, there will come heart searching that will result in cleansing from sin.

If we confess our sin, believe on the Lord Jesus Christ as Lord, and Saviour, and seek to live in the fear and love of God; we may draw near in the communion services with joy and eager anticipation. We may go to the service with confidence that there is a large measure of blessing for us.

The entire service, from the symbolical cleansing of the washing of the feet through the symbolical meal, and the conclusion in the eating of the bread and drinking of the cup, should serve to bring us into close communion with our wonderful Lord in such a way that we will be ready to go out to serve Him in newness of the life which He gives.

The Annointing of the Sick with Oil

****

CHAPTER NINE

THE CHAPTER OUTLINED:

I. Various Views

II. The Afflicted
A. The Direction Given
B. The Call of the Afflicted One
C. The Called Ones
D. The Act of Obedience
E. Illustration

III. The Healing of the Sick

SUGGESTED BACKGROUND DEVOTIONAL READING

Monday—Man That Endures Temptation (James 1:1-12)

Tuesday—"Be Ye Doers of the Word" (James 1:13-27)

Wednesday—Don't Despise the Poor (James 2:1-13)

Thursday—"Faith without Works Is Dead" (James 2:14-26)

Friday—Bridling the Tongue (James 3)

Saturday—"Draw Nigh to God" (James 4)

Sunday—God Remembers the Afflicted (James 5)

In recent years there has been a rise in the so-called *healing groups* in our nation among Protestant believers. Bold headlines in their own printed pages tell of the healings of thousands of folk from every kind of disease and infirmity. These meetings have attracted thousands of followers, and many things have been declared concerning them—some true, some untrue. We will present here, in a positive manner, what the Bible teaches relative to the subject of divine healing, and the pattern God has given to us relative to the practice of anointing the sick with oil.

As we begin this study, we suggest that you write down on paper the teachings of the Word of God as to the chief causes of the illnesses that beset us in this hour, and from which there are those who claim absolute healing if the believer has faith sufficient for the healing.

1. It is very evident from Scripture (Gen. 3) that all forms of human suffering came into the world as the result of the sin of Adam and Eve in the Garden, and of course the recurring sin in the lives of individuals. It could, therefore, be put down as a basic premise that suffering, in its original, is the result of sin.

2. Out of this basic premise, however, we need to make plain that all suffering is not the result of personal sins. However, one of the causes of suffering in the present hour is definitely the result of personal sin. Paul, in writing his first letter to the Corinthian church in relation to the sin prevalent at the Love Feast declares: "For this cause many are weak and sickly among you, and many sleep" (I Cor. 11:30). As an illustration of this particular reason, there is the case of the man who suffers from the problems of the stomach as a direct result of overindulgence of alcohol. Or again, the current picture that is being presented concerning the result of overindulgence of smoking; namely, lung cancer. Whether these are counted as sin by the world, they at least are definitely shown as contributing causes of much suffering.

3. There is another purpose suggested by Scripture for the weakness and sufferings that come upon the human race—namely, that we might comfort others in like circumstances. Again Paul writes in II Corinthians 1:4: "Who comforteth us in all our tribulation, that we may be able to comfort them which are in any trouble, by the comfort wherewith we ourselves are comforted of God."

4. There is some human suffering permitted in order that through it God may receive glory. Jesus in answering the disciples in John 9:3 answered: "Neither hath this man sinned, nor his parents: but that the works

of God should be made manifest in him." Perhaps in your own life you have seen those who have brought glory to God through their suffering. In my boyhood days we had a neighbor who was a total invalid. Though her body was wracked by pain, and though she was unable to get about the house except in her wheelchair, her very life radiated the grace and glory of God. What a Christian!

THE EXPOSITION (James 5:13-20)

Human suffering, particularly illness, has been a problem that has faced the human race for centuries. A part of the work of the Lord Jesus upon the earth was that of healing the sick. In the Book of the Acts, He continued to do that work through His followers, and we have record of many wonderful miracles of healing. But what about this period of time between the Acts of the Apostles and the return of the Lord? God has set forth His provision for us in the Epistle of James, which incidentally is the first book of the New Testament to be written. Read chapter 5, verses 13-20 of James, and ask the Holy Spirit for guidance in interpreting the passage. Now, on the other side of your paper write the list of various views held concerning this portion of God's Word.

I. VARIOUS VIEWS

1. *The Protestant view,* held by a large segment of Protestants, totally ignores the passages, relegating it to one of unimportance.

2. *The figurative view,* which explains away the meaning of this passage by interpreting it figuratively; that is, James did not have in mind physical healing, but spiritual, and that he used the physical only as an illustration.

3. *The Roman Catholic view* is that of "extreme unction," and holds it to be a rite to be performed for those about to die; hence making it a requirement of spiritual preparation before death.

4. *The dispensational view,* which limits the passage to the Jew or at least to an immediate period after the death of Christ, and to the Millennium, thus excluding any reference to our present situation as a Gentile and as the church.

5. *The inclusive view,* which is the interpretation of those who claim divine healing for all, regardless of the problem and the cause of the illness. Thus, huge lines form at healing meetings, and if the person is not cured, the healer blames the ill one for a lack of faith.

6. *The orthodox view,* and the position of the Brethren Church, is that

this passage means what it says, and that it is restricted to those who have believed in the Lord Jesus Christ and have received Him as their Saviour.

II. THE AFFLICTED (vv. 13-14)

A question is asked that sets the limits of this passage: "Is any among you afflicted?" (v. 13). "Is any sick among you?" (v. 14). Thus quickly James limits that which is to follow to "among you." There can be no doubt that he wrote this Epistle to Jews, for it opens with the words: "To the twelve tribes scattered abroad" (1:1). But a careful perusal of the book must convince the reader that these Jews were Christians. James identifies himself as "servant of God and of the Lord Jesus Christ" (v. 1), and then throughout the book identifies himself and his readers as a part of the same group. Immediately he calls them "my brethren" (v. 2), and "my beloved brethren" (v. 19), and this in a day when there was a sharp cleavage between men of the world and brethren. Persecution of the brethren began quickly after the day of Pentecost, and plagued (or blessed) the church for hundreds of years, and no such doctrine as the brotherhood of man was expounded by the early Christians. To make the break with the world meant the possibility of persecution and even death. It is true then that the book was written to Christian Jews, but we must likewise remember that the church of that day was made up almost entirely of Jews. This epistle is not limited to Jews, for the emphasis is definitely Christian, and the book itself quickly received its classification among the General Epistles of the New Testament.

The two words, "among you," which are repeated mean that the persons to whom James is giving direction are those who have been born again, and it clearly excludes those who are not a part of the body of Christ. To make this passage apply to all men everywhere is to do violence to the best interpretation of Scripture. God may heal these, but not as a result of obedience to this passage.

There is a second limitation indicated here in the use of two words, "afflicted" in verse 13, and "sick" in verse 14. The first word "afflicted" indicates the same idea as in verse 10 "suffering affliction," which simply means that there is bodily affliction that produces suffering and pain. This quickly eliminates the teaching of Christian Science and its related cousins of "theosophy" and "new thought" that bodily pain is all a matter of the mind. God recognizes human suffering and calls it by its right name. The direction here is very simple—"let him pray." The second word used is a bit stronger, "Is any sick among you?" James is now describing one who is without strength, one who is beyond the power within himself for recovery. It is the same word used in John 5:7 to describe the man who could not help himself into the pool. There it is translated "impotent"; that is, without power to do anything for himself. The conclusion must be that now James is describing an affliction of illness that is serious—bedfast or helpless as indicated by verse 15. It seems to indicate then that the directions about to be given are for ailments that are serious in their very nature. Common things that afflict us—illnesses that cause us pain, but are not dangers to permanent health should be made a matter of prayer in our own individual lives. But more serious and continuing illnesses that are afflicting us need further direction.

A. The Direction Given.

The direction given by James involves the afflicted and the elders of the church. The direction given involves prayer and anointing with oil. The direction given involves confession and faith.

B. The Call of the Afflicted One.

The service of anointing with oil begins with the call of the one who is afflicted. "Let him," that is, the sick one "call for the elders." It is not the business of the church, nor of its leadership, to announce healing services for all who will come. Neither is it the business of the church to move among the afflicted and apply for the opportunity to anoint the sick. It is the duty of the church to teach what the Word of God suggests as the way out of this affliction; hence this lesson today and the constant teaching of our pastors on this matter. The person who is seriously or continuously suffering from an illness that is not only wracking his body, but hindering his testimony and service for the Lord is to call for the elders. As a matter of fact, the verb used is one which indicates "command of the Lord"; hence, the Christian is really under orders to "call for the elders." To fail in this command would be to sin, even as to fail to carry the Gospel to the uttermost parts of the earth. The call for the anointing service should be so well understood by the church that it would be as much a part of the work of the elders as the being instant in season and out of season. The correct teaching of this part of the Bible will prevent the onslaught of so-called divine healers with their false teachings, as well as those who go to the other extreme to teach no pain.

C. The Called Ones.

There are two truths revealed in the words "elders of the church." First they are men who have been placed in prominent position in the church by the local congregation. Other passages indicate the essential requirements for this office, for example I Timothy 3:1-8, where he is referred to as "bishop" or "overseer." It is also an interesting detail that the elders are always masculine. God has chosen certain duties for the women of the church, but this is not one of their functions. Often in the case of so-called divine healers, either they are women or a woman has masterminded the program. The other truth is that the word is plural, indicating that more than one elder is to be called. This serves as a protection against the "called ones" taking unto themselves the glory that rightly belongs to the Lord. Today there are prominent men whose names are blazoned across the pages of their papers, and they are called divine healers. They lay their hands on the sick, and then pray; but God commands, "Call for the elders." When healing is effected and more than one elder participates in the anointing and praying, no one can claim the healing. How carefully God protects His name and His work.

D. The Act of Obedience.

The afflicted one having called the elders, there now remains the act of obedience on the part of both the afflicted one and the elders. (a) Confession of sin. The service should rightly begin with the confession of sin, as indicated in James 5:16, for God insists that His children be on right relationship with himself. First Corinthians 11:30 reminds us: "For this cause many are weak and sickly among you." But verses 31 and 32 follow: "For if we would judge ourselves, we should not be judged. But when we are judged, we are chastened of the Lord. . . ."

Some sickness and affliction is for the purpose of chastening, and only as we judge this sin, and confess it to the Lord does He forgive us the sin and often removes the chastening hand from upon us. (b) The anointing with oil (v. 14). The procedure follows that after confession of sin has been made, the elders shall anoint the sick with oil. The original language here gives us the direction, for it reads, "Having anointed him with oil, let them pray over him."

In our previous lesson we dealt with the symbolism of the "laying on of hands," a picture of the coming of the Holy Spirit in power at conversion, for blessing of little children, or for the work of specific tasks in the church. Now, in addition to the laying on of the hands of the elders, there is the added feature of anointing with oil. We discover again and again that oil is used as a symbol of the Holy Spirit, particularly in the Old Testament. The priests used oil in many of the functions of the Tabernacle and Temple, and a careful study of each of these indicates the express purpose in the symbol. Dr. Scofield in commenting on Zechariah 4:1-6 says: "Oil is the uniform symbol of the Spirit." This could well occupy a total study in itself. Let us again stress the fact that there is no efficacy in the oil. However, God has commanded that the symbol of the Holy Spirit be included in the service, and to conduct a service of this kind without oil is a distinct disobedience to the command of the Lord.

Let us likewise stress the truth that this does not set aside the fact that God uses doctors, nurses, and medicine to bring about healing. One thing is sure that every means should be employed that is good for the healing of the sick person.

Dr. Hoyt suggests that it is "good theology, that while God may will and order the end, He also provides a means to reach the end. In some cases, He may use the doctor." (c) The name of the Lord (v. 14). The anointing is always done in the name of the Lord. Here again, we believe that the Scriptures are very careful even in the use of the names of our Saviour. The word "Lord" carries with it the implication of total authority. The service itself is commanded by the Lord, and when we in obedience to the command, follow the instructions, it includes the fact that the entire situation is placed in His hands. There is the evidence that the elders who have come to share in the service recognize that all healing is of the Lord, and if the sick is healed, it is not by their hands, or by the oil that they use, or even by the prayers which they pray, but by the power of the Lord conveyed through His Holy Spirit. It also involves the fact that the elders and the sick one esteem the will of the Lord above everything else that happens. If God wills to heal, then blessed be the name of the Lord. If He chooses not to heal, then blessed be the name of the Lord, for He is the Lord of the universe.

The Apostle Paul faced it in a very real sense when He said: "For this thing I besought the Lord thrice, that it might depart from me. And he said unto me, My grace is sufficient for thee: for my strength is made perfect in weakness . . ." (II Cor. 12:8-9). (d) The prayer for the sick (v. 14). This prayer follows the anointing, and comes while the elders remain with their hands upon the sick. Much ought to be said concerning this prayer, but a part of it has already been intimated above. The very language used indicates that it must be a prayer of worship and devotion. One in which the Lord shall be exalted, and the power of the Lord declared. It is a prayer that recognizes the plan of God which includes every individual, as well as the whole universe. It recognizes that the Lord of the universe is "all wise"; therefore, whatever He does in relation to the sick, He will not nor can He, make any mistake. It is a prayer which recognizes the will of the Lord, rather than the demands or desires of the ones gathered in the sick room. How contrary this idea is to that of the so-called faith healers of the present hour who literally *demand* that God heal the individual.

E. Illustration.

I watched a so-called faith healer one afternoon on television as he actually demanded that God heal a young lady of an ailment in her feet. After the *healing* had taken place (which we questioned), he asked her: "Now that God has healed you, what are you going to do?" The young lady replied: "Go back to my job dancing in the nightclub for which I am working." Needless so say, the ushers quickly hurried the young lady off the platform and away from the television cameras, and it was easy to see that the "healer" was upset by the answer which she gave. If we could add one more word concerning the prayer for the sick, it would be that in this entire passage the emphasis seems to be upon the prayer for the sick in contrast to the anointing with oil. The anointing with oil should be a part of the service, but in reality the church is urged to pray with the elders for the healing of the sick.

III. THE HEALING OF THE SICK (v. 15)

There are several things in the healing of the sick which we need to note, for each has its bearing upon the entire picture.

1. "The Lord shall raise him up" (v. 15). First of all, it is the Lord himself who is the source of all healing. This is true regardless of what medium is used, or what prayer may be offered in behalf of the sick. It is His prerogative to heal immediately and without the aid of any means whatsoever, or do so as He chooses through the service mentioned here, or through doctors and medicine. It is His prerogative to heal at some subsequent time or never.

2. "The prayer of faith" is the designated means by which the healing comes, for He says: "And the prayer of faith shall save the sick" (v. 15). One additional fact should be pointed out about this prayer; namely, that it is a prayer that is wrought by God himself within the elders. Verse 16

makes this conclusion essential when in its best translation it reads: "The prayer of a righteous man, which is being wrought within him, accomplishes much." This makes God the very one who gives the elders the prayer which they pray, and such prayer gets results.

3. "Save the sick" (v. 15). This simply means deliverance from sickness, and thus points to the healing of the body. What a glorious thing it is to know that in response to obedience, God often chooses to heal our loved ones and to raise them up for further service to His glory.

THE CONCLUSION (vv. 19-20)

In the final two verses of the book, the apostle sets forth the ultimate purpose in the service of anointing and prayer. It is to reach and deal with sins in the lives of the saints. While sin may or may not be the cause of the sickness at hand, the anointing service gives the sick person an opportunity to be brought nearer to the Lord.

James reminds us of the possibility of all of God's children erring from the path of His way for our lives (v. 19). He points out the direction of all error, that it is first from the truth, and then follows in conduct. To convert, or turn such a one around is the privilege and the responsibility of every member of the body of Christ. Often, severe illness is the means God uses to get this job of conversion done.

The immediate effect of converting such a one is that he will be saved immediately from his doctrinal error. This means that his life will be changed and sins which would have come as a result of his failure in doctrine will not be committed. But the ultimate of it all is that this one will be saved from physical and eternal death.

In an hour when the world is looking for a solution through all manner of false healers, the church of Jesus Christ should take opportunity to teach the truth of God's Word concerning this as well as all other matters.

Nonresistance in War and Peace

****

CHAPTER TEN

THE CHAPTER OUTLINED:

I. The Biblical Background
Spiritual Principles Established

II. The Doctrine of Nonresistance
A. Nonresistance in War
B. Nonresistance in Peace

SUGGESTED BACKGROUND DEVOTIONAL READING

Monday—The Believer Characterized (Matt. 5:1-12)

Tuesday—The Believer's Influence (Matt. 5:13-16)

Wednesday—The Spirit of the Law (Matt. 5:38-48)

Thursday—Outworking of Christian Life (Rom. 12:9-21)

Friday—Responsibility to the State (Rom. 13:1-7)

Saturday—Responsibility to Society (Rom. 13:8-14)

Sunday—Settling Disputes (I Cor. 6:1-11)

Our task as Christians is not to make the government, or to meddle in the government. Thank God for the government we have, and this could be said of most any kind of government, for I am convinced that any government, even the weakest and most corrupt, is better than none at all. For apart from government, there would be anarchy, and any government is better than anarchy. But I am a Christian, and I must find God's answer for myself while I am passing through this world.

Because we are citizens of the United States there are certain requirements laid upon us, one of which is the registration of every young man indicating his military status. In our day there have been some young men who have rebelled against the call of their country, and by the public burning of their draft cards they have shown open rebellion to the call to serve in the service of the United States of America. Does the Bible issue instructions regarding responsibility to God and to our country?

I. THE BIBLICAL BACKGROUND

Since the Bible is the basis of every action for the Christian, it is essential as we begin the study of this subject of *nonresistance* that we shall discover what God has said in His Word that is appropriate to this subject.

Spiritual Principles Established (Matt. 5:38-48).

In the teaching of our Lord in this entire section, it is generally agreed that He was setting forth the pattern of life for the Kingdom of God, which would be established upon the earth during the millennial reign. It has been suggested, and we believe rightly so, that this entire section will actually become the constitution of the kingdom when it is established. However, the application of these as spiritual principles must be made in the present, for when a man is born again, he actually becomes a citizen of the kingdom and ought to begin to practice the principles of that government in the present hour.

1. *The principle is contrasted* with that of former laws established by the Old Testament, for Jesus suggests in verse 38: "Ye have heard that it hath been said, An eye for an eye, and a tooth for a tooth," which was but a part of the principle of justice established by the law (Exod. 21:23-25). As we study that law, we discover that very strict retaliation was permitted under the law through the proper courts of justice.

Now as we turn to the statement of the Lord Jesus, let us be reminded that He was not drawing up a set of laws for the state of His day. His teaching was not to any legislative body. He spoke to men who were living under a very stern yoke of government—the Roman yoke. His words made no impact upon the leaders of that government, nor were they intended to make any impact upon those leaders. Without doubt the words of Jesus, "But I say unto you, That ye resist not evil: but whosoever shall smite thee on thy right cheek, turn to him the other also" (Matt. 5:39), were primarily given for private conduct.

The principle did not concern the question of the state's duty in defending its coast from invasion, or protecting its citizens by police supervision from crime and criminals. The other contrast has been made that Jesus was establishing now a new principle not only for the individual, but also the state. We dare not narrow the function of the principle, but surely the teaching is that so long as the state is not Christian, Christian principles cannot be looked for in legislation. Of course, when the kingdom of God comes upon the earth its people will be subjects of the King, the Lord of lords; hence these rules can justly apply.

2. *The principle enjoins the Christian* to live without attempt at vengeance. The whole law to which Jesus referred was that ". . . vengeance is mine; I will repay saith the Lord" (Rom. 12:19, cf. Deut. 32:35). Again, remember, Jesus said, ". . . whosoever shall smite thee . . . turn to him the other [cheek] also . . . if any man will sue thee at the law, . . . let him have thy cloke also" (Matt. 5:39-40). This is consistent with law and order. It in no way concerns the civil rights of anyone other than the Christian himself. The policeman on the beat is required by law to guard the citizen from unlawful attack, but the Christian is not expected to take revenge for an attack against his own person. The Scriptures ask that the Christian "resist evil" in the correct manner, for we are told to "Put on the whole armour of God, that ye may be able to stand against the wiles of the devil," but here we are advised by our Lord not to use physical force to resist evil or the evil one.

By saying "resist not evil," let us remember that Christ did not say that we could not, or should not, avoid evil. He himself went from Judea into Galilee to avoid the resentment of the Pharisees (John 4:1-3), and He instructed His disciples that when persecution should arise against them in one city, they should pass on to another city (Matt. 10:23). He does not say that we cannot resist it within certain limitations (John 18:23), but here He is teaching against the law of retaliation. This law must be in consistency with the law of love, which He is about to set forth. This is best gained by real forgiveness.

3. *The positive principle is set forth in three areas.*

a. When the Christian suffers bodily injury, represented in this case by a blow upon the cheek. This is a slap at the status of the individual, and a blow upon the physical, but Jesus reminds us that it must be borne with patience, even offering the other cheek. Jesus set the example for this, for even though He was and is the Great Judge of the universe, when smitten, He did not smite again (John 18:23). Remember, that generally not to "smite again" will avoid a quarrel. It is the return blow that makes the quarrel.

b. When the Christian suffers loss to property represented in this case by the loss of a coat. The rule established is that the Christian may suffer wrong through those who make no pretense of honesty, and may lose a coat. Here they shall give their cloak, rather than go to law. The cost of both may be less than the cost of the lawsuit. In addition, going to court may cost you the opportunity of winning that one to Christ.

c. When the Christian suffers loss of liberty is represented by the fact that Jesus says: "Whosoever shall compel thee to go with him a mile, go with him twain" (Matt. 5:41). Personal liberties are often taken away by unscrupulous employers, by unchristian companions, and by leaders in every realm of life. When this is done, Jesus reminds us that we are to bear the hardships patiently without fighting back, "go . . . twain" says He, rather than contend or be contentious.

II. THE DOCTRINE OF NONRESISTANCE

Having firmly established the Biblical basis for our discussion, we come now to discover the position of the Brethren Church in relation to these Biblical passages. Dr. Hoyt in his book *All Things* has divided the subject into two major parts; namely, "Nonresistance in War," and "Nonresistance in Peace." We shall follow these two in our further study.

A. Nonresistance in War.

The doctrine is set forth clearly in the statement of the annual conference as set forth in the statement of October 29, 1949, which reads: "That we reaffirm our historic position with regard to war; namely, 'that the Brethren Church from her origin has maintained that the use of violence or physical force, as a means to an end, on the part of God's children, is contrary to Holy Writ.' "

This statement, and the doctrine of nonresistance does not make the

Brethren Church and its members pacifists. The extreme pacifist movements of the day are encouraged largely by those who would apply the teachings of Jesus to all, including unsaved individuals as well as nations. Jesus did not make this mistake. Of course, there are some who follow extreme pacifism; not because Jesus taught it, but because they are involved in giving allegiance to communism.

Neither does this doctrine make its members "in rebellion against the government." It does insist that Christians ought not to use violence, fighting with carnal weapons, or even with their hands against an enemy. The Christian will on the other hand be subject to his government in every possible manner, where it does not cause him to violate the higher commandment of God. He will be willing to enter the service of the government in time of war, to minister to the needs of those who are maimed, or to supply the physical strength essential to those fighting the battles. He himself will not be involved in the battle. The government recognizes this and in days past has given privilege to Christians of what is commonly referred to as "noncombatant service," which may involve him in any one of many duties, none of which means he must carry arms, or fight in the battle. To accuse the Christian of being cowardly to take this position is to misunderstand the position itself, for it takes more courage humanly speaking to withstand the evil of a battle and not fight back, than to go out with revenge in the heart. Men who stand in noncombatant service are faced with all of the dangers of other soldiers with the additional fact that they are unarmed. Often, under heavy fire, the noncombatant becomes the man sent into the fire to bring back the wounded and dying. Christians should take this position because it is here that they can do most for their government and for their fellow men by giving assistance in the moral and spiritual realms under heavy pressures of the world forces of evil.

Let us make sure that we understand the doctrine so that we may help others to know its true meaning. This doctrine does not state that "war is wrong for civil governments." The Bible does teach that physical force for the Christian is wrong, but governments are not Christian. The very nature of the governments of this world, and their constituency demand that they be defended. Perhaps the finest commentary on the entire subject is that of the Apostle Paul to the Romans when in Romans 13:4 he says: ". . . But if thou do that which is evil, be afraid; for he beareth not the sword in vain: for he is the minister of God, a revenger to execute wrath upon him that doeth evil." Carnal weapons, and the use of them by governments is never said to be evil for this generation of unbelievers. Arbitration and treaties are good, and ought to be used as far as possible to avoid warfare, and carnal weapons, but there finally comes a time when these are no longer possible, and the only answer is to the use of physical force.

One other truth that needs to be made sure is that war will continue until the end of time. The Bible never teaches that the day will come when civil governments will cease their fightings. As a matter of fact, Christ reminds us that there will be wars and rumors of wars until the end of time, and this is supported by every prophecy of the end times (cf. Dan. 9:26; Joel 3:9-12; Rev. 19:11-21). Therefore, it will be essential that governments shall continue to defend themselves with armies, navy fleets, air flights, and even atomic weapons, or others of worse nature to prevent the enemy from taking over.

Since it is right for the government to wage war, and to use carnal weapons to fight its battles, and since the Bible teaches that it is right to obey the government in things that are right, some may come to the conclusion that Christians ought, therefore, to fight in wars and use the weapons of war as provided by the government. But the Bible teaches as a principle that Christians are subject to a power higher than the government, and when things do not agree between the two, the Christian must always be subject to the higher—that is the law of God (Acts 4:19-20; 5:29).

APPLICATION OF THIS TRUTH

What then is the attitude of the church and of the individual in a generation in which all young men are expected to register for military service, and be subject to call? The church has the responsibility to teach what the Bible has to say about nonresistance, and its application to the individual. It likewise has the responsibility to teach the provision the government has made for those who are Christian, and who hold to a nonresistance, or noncombatant position. It does not indicate to individuals in this matter any more than in any other matter of choice. It provides the teaching, prays for those who must make the decisions, and then regardless of the position they take in relation to this teaching, they continue to care for, nurture, and follow them with love through whatever crisis may come. The individual Christian must make this a matter of careful study in the Word of God, and then under the direction of the

Spirit of God, make an honest decision by which he stands. The decision should be one of personal conviction, and not made because of a position which the church takes.

B. Nonresistance in Peace.

Perhaps this is an area even more difficult than that of nonresistance in war or military service. The Scriptures covering the relation of believers in settling disputes between themselves and other believers and likewise nonbelievers seem to be clear. They are not many in number, but one such direction should be sufficient.

1. *The relation of believers with believers in settling disputes* (I Cor. 6:1-11). Paul begins by suggesting that to go to law before an unjust (that is an unsaved or worldly) court is nothing short of insubordination before God. He tells us why, for the saved are to judge the world when the time of judgment shall come. God has exalted the church to the most exalted position in the world, that of judging the world. If God has deemed the church to be worthy of this high position, how dare we go to an unsaved court of justice to settle our little disputes? Actually, Paul goes beyond this to declare that to take a brother to court was to be guilty of sin (vv. 6-8). The charge against the Corinthian Christians was simply that they were guilty of fraud, of robbing their fellow believers. The courts simply provided for them a legal way of stealing from their brethren that which did not belong to them. The section which follows this is indeed a strong blast against all manner of sin, and Paul seems to be accusing them of following some of this type of sin in their own lives. The truth is that Paul says the very fact that they are guilty of going to law seems to point the finger of question upon them as to whether they have really been saved.

There is a way to settle disputes between members of the body of Christ (I Cor. 6:4-7). The passage clearly indicates that there are differences that need to be settled, and that there are wrongs that need to be made right. But there is only one place that this should and dares to be done; namely, within the church. There ought to be at least one wise man before whom such matters could be arbitrated. There should be at least one to whom you dare look for an impartial judgment upon the matter. But, if there cannot be found even one person who will hear the matter, and render an impartial judgment, what then? Paul answers it clearly in the subject of our lesson for today; namely, nonresistance. "Why do ye not rather take wrong? why do ye not suffer yourselves to be defrauded?" (v. 7).

We preach that "Christ is the answer to every problem," but somehow seem to confine it to the people who are unsaved in an appeal to get them saved. If Christ is all that we preach and believe Him to be, then surely there ought to be a definite waiting before the Lord in every problem in the local church and in the problems of our church across the nation. Christ is the answer and we must wait upon Him, leaving Him to give to us peaceful solutions to the differences between individual Christians and between bodies of believers.

2. *The relation of believers with nonbelievers in settling disputes* (Matt. 5:39-40). Often, the argument is heard that when Christians go into court, it is against the unbelievers, and, therefore, we have a right to treat them as heathen, taking action against them in the worldly courts. But let us come back again to the original passage of study for the day. Jesus said: "But I say unto you, Resist not him that is evil" (Matt. 5:39 ASV). Some have held that this refers to Satan himself, but this would be contrary to the Scriptures, and is not in keeping with the context. The words which follow "whosoever" (v. 39), "any man" (v. 40), and "whosoever" (v. 41) suggest that the whole matter about which Jesus is talking is beyond the confines of the church and her membership. If the man would take you to law, and sue for your coat, let him have thy cloak also (v. 40). You say this is going too far? Remember, God is the one to whom vengeance belongs, and He has the last word to say. Jesus does not intimate that this will be an easy road for the Christian. He does not say that it will be a decision that will come at the instant of the new birth. But this is the direction of choice the Christian ought to take as he matures in the things of Christ. But in addition to this negative position—that of nonresistance—in going to law with an unbeliever, we are even directed to take a further step and "give him thy cloke also," which is to say, give him more than he asked for, and demonstrate the righteousness of Christ which is shed abroad in your life by exceeding the demands of the law. To go the second mile, or to follow willingly when liberty has been taken away, will often heap coals of fire upon the head of the unbeliever, and in so doing, demonstrate that truly Jesus Christ is the answer to the problems of the world.

APPLICATION OF THIS TRUTH

There are many areas where this great truth of nonresistance in the world can be applied. It is not just a matter of "not going to court" to settle disputes. The doctrine of nonresistance is learning to live in our neighborhoods as peaceful citizens, not raising our voices against injustices that may be done. It is learning to work at our jobs as good employees without becoming ensnarled in the movements against employers even though injustices may be done. Nonresistance is living together as a family, even though one or more members of the family may be unsaved, and not willing to be the kind of family citizens that make for the happiest home. It is suffering for the cause of Christ, even as He suffered, without opening our mouths in reviling and backbiting against the one who inflicts the suffering upon us.

There is perhaps no harder word written for the Christian than that of "Resist not . . . evil . . .," but it is written, and to manifest nonresistance is ours to follow under His direction, and by His spirit so that God may receive the glory, and His name published abroad in all the earth.

In commenting on this entire matter, Dr. Campbell Morgan said: "Oh, this ethic of Jesus, how it scorches! . . . This ethic of Jesus, which does not express itself in small rules, but in great principles; not in a decalogue in stone, but in a requirement in the heart, is the severest thing that the world has ever had."

To follow this injunction of our Lord will mean to receive the jeers of the crowd, and perhaps even to lose prestige in the world, but to gain the blessing of God for obedience to His will and His Word.

Separation from the World

****

CHAPTER ELEVEN

THE CHAPTER OUTLINED:

I. Biblical Basis of the Doctrine
A. The Persons Involved in Separation
B. The Principle of Separation Commanded
C. The Provision Made for Separation

II. Some General Considerations
A. Concerning the Right or Wrong Decision
B. In Making the Decision
C. Matter of Separation from the World

SUGGESTED BACKGROUND DEVOTIONAL READING

Monday—Love Not the World (I John 2:12-17)

Tuesday—Overcoming the World (I John 5:1-5)

Wednesday—The Kingdoms of the World (Matt. 4:1-11)

Thursday—Friendship of the World (James 4:1-10)

Friday—Deserter Loved the World (II Tim. 4:9-18)

Saturday—Escaping the Corruption (II Peter 1:1-4)

Sunday—Pollutions of the World (II Peter 2:9-22)

Christian leaders are constantly besieged with questions concerning the conduct of the Christian life. "May I do this as a Christian?" When the answer is given there is always a second question that follows, "Why?" This is not a problem that has come with the present generation, but was faced by the apostles at the beginning of the church. The difficulty has often been in the fact that men have attempted to establish rules of conduct for the church without putting down basic foundations of Biblical teaching for those rules of conduct. As a result, the questions continue to fall from the lips of Christians everywhere.

On a piece of paper draw an outline picture of a modern building above which write the words, "The Christian Life." Now note some of the problems which you and your friends may be concerned about in the every day living of the Christian life. Use these subjects as the titles of the "building blocks" which you now draw on the outline of the building. Such problems might include: conduct, dress, speech, companions, and so on. When the building is completed; that is, when you have listed a number of the problems, remember to add the basic necessity; namely, the foundation. Beneath the building, draw a foundation, which is the basis of our current study: "Biblical teaching of separation from the world."

I. BIBLICAL BASIS OF THE DOCTRINE (I John 2:12-17; 5:1-5)

The Brethren Church was born in a period that was known as "The Pietistic Movement" in church history. This movement has often been called a second reformation because it insisted that true Christian life should evolve as a direct result of real Christian faith. Frequently, in our own generation and among evangelical believers of many branches of Christendom, this has been referred to as the doctrine of separation.

A. The Persons Involved in Separation (I John 2:12-14).

A part of the problem in the total doctrine arises out of the fact that often people who are not "born again" are attempting to live as Christians and hence are struggling.

The Apostle John guards well the doctrine as he writes the preface to the command itself by addressing various persons. (a) They are addressed first of all in a general manner, when he says: "I write unto you, little children" (vv. 12-13). There are two separate words used in the original language which are translated "little children." In verse 12, a literal translation would read, "dear children," and expresses the heart of the apostle as he writes to all of "his flock" in terms of endearment and affection. "Little ones" is the literal translation of the word in verse 13, and we see here the idea of subordination to someone above.

Two general ideas then are involved: First, these to whom he writes are members of the great family of God because of the new birth. Second, as members of the family, they recognize the authority God has over them, and likewise as little children, their utter dependence upon Him as their Heavenly Father. (b) In addition to this general way of addressing the believers, he moves to a more particular direction in talking to them according to their degree of experience in the Christian life.

There are the "fathers," composed of older members of the body of believers, who have become ripe with experience and mature in the faith. There are the "young men" (vv. 13-14) who are active in the service of the Lord in whom the full vigor and strength of manhood surges forth to battle against the enemy. (c) He writes to these because of experiences which have been theirs. Without these experiences, there would be no basis for separation from the world—the experience of forgiven sins (v. 12).

The message of the Gospel has been proclaimed, and these have heard and believed. As a result of that belief, their sins are forgiven. From that moment until the present the believer has the blessed experience of freedom from the guilt of sin. This is the only foundation upon which to teach separation from the world. (d) The experience of knowing the Father (v. 13). As a result of believing, sins having been forgiven, these have been brought into the family of God and now said to know fully the Father— not in the sense of knowing all there is to know about Him, but rather to know in the fullest sense, the experience of forgiveness, of cleansing, of His love.

B. The Principle of Separation Commanded (I John 2:15-17).

Because John has now settled for us the persons involved, he is now ready to set forth the command, which basically sets forth the principle of *separation.* "Love not the world, neither the things that are in the world" is a very simple statement.

It states the principle clearly. Now we will begin to analyze it carefully. In the small space of three verses, John repeats the word "world" five times. Before we can understand the command God has issued, we must understand what we are "not to love." In his book, *All Things,* Dr. Hoyt points out that much of the confusion over this word arises from the fact that four different words in the original of the New Testament are translated at one time or another by the same English word "world," and yet each of these words designate something different. *Ge* is the first word and is used but once in the New Testament, and, although translated by the word "world," it actually has reference to earth or land (cf. Rev. 13:3). In the American Standard Version, and others that have come since the King James Version, the word is more correctly translated by the term "whole earth." This is not the word with which we are dealing, when John commands "Love not the world." *Oikoumene* is a second word which is translated "world," and appears fifteen times in the New Testament.

In every case except one it is the English word "world" and in that case (Luke 21:26) it is translated "earth." It actually refers to the inhabited part of the earth, and in the days of the New Testament was synonomous with the Roman Empire as for example in Luke 2:1. Again, this word is not the "world" that John is dealing with when he says: "Love not the world." *Aion* is a third word translated in some cases by the word "world," although here there are many other words used to describe or translate; for example, ever, evermore, eternal, ages, world. The word actually carries a time element in it, and means an age or a period of time, the length depending upon the context in which it is used. Here again we would simply say John was not talking about this when he issued the command. *Kosmos* is the fourth word, and is the word of our text, when John says "Love not the world [kosmos]."

A detailed study of this word is important at this point if we are to fully know John's meaning. Perhaps the finest way that we can catch the significance of the word is to look at several Biblical illustrations of its use, and from them draw the truth. In I Peter 3:3 the word "kosmos" is translated "adorning," and actually refers to the arrangement or fashion of material substance. "Whose adorning let it not be that outward adorning of plaiting the hair, and wearing of gold, or of putting on of apparel." It is very evident that Peter was not forbidding the "plaiting of hair" or "the wearing of gold." If that be true, then he was likewise forbidding the "wearing of apparel," and, of course, this is completely contrary to all that we know of the Bible. He does say that these—including the wearing of apparel—are not to be the adornment of the woman. This is a spiritual matter, an inward adornment. Thus it will be seen that the word means arrangement, or fashion.

Sometimes the matter of arrangement, or fashion, is not confined to material substance, but can include even the very ideas that prevail in a given society, or culture of people. It may relate itself in every realm—education, religion, government, financial, recreational, and amusement. Yet it need not be confined to these ideas, but likewise may extend to the realities, such as the fashion or arrangement in cities, churches, people. The very movement of a divided chancel and the use of two pulpits in a church, which is so prevalent in our day, is for some a "conforming to the fashion of the day," although to others it may be useful because of the liturgy that is followed by that fellowship of churches. I heard a prominent architect in the United States condemn this from the viewpoint that a divided chancel was not in keeping for certain of the churches represented in the conference, since their theological beliefs did not correspond with the program of a divided chancel.

The argument was an architectural argument on nonconformity simply because there was no basic reason for conformity to the divided chancel program now so much in vogue. A second word about this is found in I John 2:17 where the word is used in conjunction with the ideas of an ending, "the world passeth away." This means that the present fashion, or order of things is in a constant state of flux. There is never a moment when the arrangement of things as we know them today is not in this constant state of flux. Our own generation has witnessed the passing away of governments perhaps more than any other age in the history of the world.

This does not mean that the material of the world, the earth is passing away. The land is still there, the people still live on the land, but the government under which they lived may have changed two or three times in a single generation. One other idea is evident in the word "kosmos," for it is the basic word from which we get our word "cosmetic," which is the word used in our day to describe those material aids that are supposed to make an individual more attractive or beautiful. Hence, when John saw the word "kosmos" with its basic root meaning, he intends to indicate to us that the world has a certain attractiveness about it that draws the heart away from the realities of God. It matters little what part of the world you occupy, there will be an attractiveness there for you. If your interests are in the financial world, there will be the attractiveness of the stock market, bonds, banks, money.

If your interests are industrial, then, of course, the attraction will be machines and buildings and production. If a housewife at home, it may be the beauty and comforts of the house, and the security that you find there behind closed doors and drawn draperies. If your world centers around the intellectual, of course the attraction will include more and more of education and degrees attached to your name. Having discovered the true meaning of the word "world," we move now to discover just what a Christian is to do concerning the world, and John sums it up in two little words, "love not."

Many at this point have been confused because the command comes in words of the negative. As a result at least three false positions have arisen which must be faced early in the study: (1) Monasticism. Some have felt that in order to abide by the teaching of John and other portions of the Word of God, it is essential that the Christian withdraw from the world of people, and move into a monastery.

How often have you heard people say: "Wouldn't it be wonderful to move away from it all?" Perhaps it is safe to say that everyone of us hates sin to the place where we would like to get away from it all with its sordidness and suffering, but moving to a monastery does not remove us from sin, it only puts us into a different class of society, and a different kind of *kosmos*. Two passages of Scripture bear on this particularly; namely, John 17:5 when Jesus prayed that His followers not be taken out of the world but that they should be kept from the evil. The other, when Paul exhorts his followers in Corinth (I Cor. 5:9-10), to separate company with certain men, yet not altogether, for ". . . then must ye needs go out of the world." (2) Asceticism is a second danger that has arisen out of the teaching of this command. This is a life of practicing certain codes of life, rules laid down by men whereby they hope to attain to deep spirituality.

Paul deals with it in Colossians 2:21-23, where he sets forth some of the things established, such as "touch not; taste not; handle not." The problem of course arises out of the fact that there are not rules enough to meet every situation of life, and no philosophy fulfills every need of the human heart. Let us remember that from that day until the present, the desire of human philosophy and philosophers has been to draw the minds and hearts away from the supernatural, and from God to themselves. (3) Ritualism is the third danger, and because it is so much a part of religion, it has become very effective in drawing men from Christ. This is the careful observance of days, ordinances, rites for the sake of these things themselves and not so much for what they symbolize or teach. Again, Paul writes to the Colossians (Col. 2:16-20), warning them of the dangers of this belief. The devil is still actively engaged in getting the attention of people focused upon the symbol to leave the real subject of worship; namely, our wonderful Lord.

This admonition of John is in the negative, "love not," but it is only another way of saying: Whoever loves the Father must be constantly separating himself from the world and the things that are in the world. This is consistent with the content of Scripture elsewhere. The Apostle Paul, in Colossians 3:2 says: "Set your affection on things above, not on things on the earth." James, in his Epistle (4:4), says: "Ye adulterers and adulteresses, know ye not that the friendship of the world [kosmos] is enmity with God?"

Dr. George G. Findlay in his book, *Fellowship in the Life Eternal,* says: "The world [kosmos] is a bewildering paradox; each man bears in his own breast the mirror of the contradiction, its counterpart is little. It is the sphere at once of light and darkness, heaven and hell; the divine and the satanic wrestle there for mastery, and their forms are confused in the struggle. The world is at once to be loved and loathed: to be loved as God made it and Christ redeemed it; to be loathed and feared as sin has marred it, as the serpent has drawn over it his trail and charged it with his venom."

The reasons for the command. Before John leaves the command, he sets forth God's reasons for this command, and any of these three would be sufficient.

(1) He says: "If any man love the world, the love of the Father is not in him" (v. 15). Where the love of God does not abide as the ruling authority in life, there is but darkness. It is interesting to note here that John places "love of the world" in direct antithesis to "love of the Father." Both cannot live in the same soul. There can be no peaceful coexistence. When the love of the Father comes into the human soul, it drives from that soul evil affections and lusts that war against the soul. This kind of love binds the lover to the object of his love. Here is the secret of overcoming the present trend in the church toward worldliness. It is not a worked up enthusiasm of moving against evil trends, but rather a deepening love that grows in the soul of the lover moment by moment.

(2) Love of the world is not of the Father, for all "that is in the world, the lust of the flesh, and the lust of the eyes, and the pride of life, is not of the Father." This says simply that the very makeup of the things that are in the world make it impossible for the child of God to love the world as an end in themselves. The lust of the flesh involves and includes all bodily desires that go beyond the limits set for them. There is a legitimate and

necessary expression of bodily desires, but when they break through the limitations established, and absorb the mind and fill the heart to the complete control of the individual, then the desires have swollen into lust. The lust of the eyes signifies a different type of testing that comes. It is in the realm of aesthetic sensibilities and is beyond the mere bodily appetites. Here again is a God-given privilege to enjoy through the eye gate all of the beauties of the world. But this God-given privilege may be prostituted and profaned, and give way to bewitching perils and corruption of satanic glory.

(3) The pride of life is without doubt the most subtle and devastating form of testing which the devil is able to promote. Here is the ultimate in conceit, in the pride of possessions whether they be material or symbolic of success in every field. This can come as a testing to the pastor, layman, or teacher even in the work of the Lord. The final reason given by John is that of the passing of the world (v. 17). The world is passing away, therefore, men ought not to love the world.

C. The Provision Made for Separation (I John 5:1-5).

The very wonderful thing about every command that God has given to man is that He has provided the way whereby that command may be accomplished. So here, we discover that there is sufficient provision. (a) It begins with new life in Jesus Christ: "Whosoever believeth that Jesus is the Christ is born of God . . ." (5:1). Jesus himself said that this cannot come of one's self, but only by the Spirit of God. There is a new love that comes to replace the old love. The Son of God is the center of attraction, and He is that One who fills the heart with new affection. (b) It continues with an obedience to the will of God (vv. 2-3). Let us remember that the commandments of God are summed up in the commandment of love. To the unregenerate heart, the keeping of the commandments is impossible, but to the regenerate heart, the new affection drives sinful desires and thoughts away, and places in their stead a program that pleases God and ennobles character. (c) There is victory provided for "whatsoever is born of God overcometh the world." Paul writes: "We are more than conquerors," and yet it is not in our own strength, or our own ability, but rather through faith in the Son of God. "This is the victory . . . even our faith." Not a faith in everything that comes along, nor in governments of this world, or in leagues, but in the Son of God. Dr. B. F. Westcott declares: "While victory was gained upon a narrow battlefield, the hill called Calvary, yet it was worldwide in its extent. It continues to be effective today." He who loves God and exercises personal faith in the Son of God is given this conquering faith against which no weapon ever forged by Satan can succeed.

II. SOME GENERAL CONSIDERATIONS

With all that has been said concerning the general subject of separation, it may be helpful to set forth some ideas to guide each of us:

A. Concerning the Right or Wrong Decision.

The individual should be sure that the decision is motivated by genuine conviction in view of clearly established facts from the Word of God, and not by a passing fancy or rule. Otherwise the decision will not last long.

B. In Making the Decision.

In making the decision, particularly as it relates to "separation from fellowship" of certain individuals, be sure that it is more than a mere clash of personalities. It is so easy to allow hurt pride, jealousy, personal dislike, thwarted personal ambition, and the like to prompt one in a desire for separation from other individuals within the church, or denomination.

C. Matter of Separation from the World.

As you think of the matter of separation from the world, remember there is a vast difference in contending for the faith, and being contentious. As one great Christian leader expressed it: "There is a difference between contending for the faith and contending with the faithful."

Consistent in All Things

✳✳✳✳✳✳✳✳✳✳✳✳✳✳✳✳✳✳✳✳✳✳✳✳✳✳✳✳✳✳✳✳✳✳

CHAPTER TWELVE

THE CHAPTER OUTLINED:

I. The Doctrine Stated

II. The Doctrine Pictured
  A. Separation in Custom
  B. Separation in Company
  C. Separation in Conduct

III. The Doctrine in Practical Application
  A. Religion
  B. Speech
  C. Dress
  D. Pleasure
  E. Family Life
  F. Social Life

IV. Consistency in Nonconformity

SUGGESTED BACKGROUND DEVOTIONAL READINGS

Monday—Christian Transformation (Rom. 12:1-5)

Tuesday—Transformed Conduct (Col. 3:12-25)

Wednesday—A Changed Life Puzzles the World (I Peter 4:1-9)

Thursday—The Will of God (I Thess. 4:1-12)

Friday—Put Off the Old Man (Eph. 4:20-32)

Saturday—Be Doers of the Word (James 1:21-27)

Sunday—God's Enablement (I Cor. 10:12-20)

If one word more than any other describes the age in which we live, it is the word "conformity." Everyone is doing it; therefore it must be right! There is a mad race that is demanding that everyone keep up with their next-door neighbor in every aspect of life. Status in the community has become the most important area to most people. The spirit of the age has gotten into individual lives until now men are bankrupting themselves financially, spiritually, morally, and just about every other way that could be mentioned in order to keep up with the Jones family next door. An article in a popular magazine reported the greatest desire of high school students was to be accepted, and this demanded conformity.

In the previous chapter, as we studied the basic foundation of this matter of separation from the world, we suggested the drawing of a building, and the naming of some of the areas that were problems—these to become the names on the building blocks. Let us come today with a quick review of the basic foundation in order that we may deal with the individual matters that are involved in being consistent in all things.

There is a story told by Dr. C. F. Yoder that would introduce this study directly which follows: "There was once a poor family which moved from Chicago to a small village. The two little girls entered school with cheap, red calico dresses, but the other children made fun of their dresses, and they came home crying. Their mother said to them, 'Go back again and tell the other girls that we did not come here to follow style, but to set the style.' They did as they were told, and lo, it was not long until the other little girls in the school appeared in red calico dresses also." So should it be with the Christian. He is not in the world to follow the style, but to set the style. He has received a new life and now must manifest it to the world.

I. THE DOCTRINE STATED (Rom. 12:1-2)

When we begin to deal with the subject of consistency in separation, we are faced with many different ideas concerning the subject. To talk of this doctrine in general is a very simple matter, but to define it and narrow it down to specifics causes everyone to come face to face with the very heart of the Christian walk. The simplest statement of the entire doctrine is that given to the church at Rome by the Apostle Paul, when he said: "Be not conformed to this world: but be ye transformed . . ." (Rom. 12:2). A better translation of the word "conformed" would be fashioned, and would read: Be not fashioned after this world. One of the reasons that it has been difficult to write down all that is involved in the fashion of this world is because the fashion of this world is a changing thing. When we say of anything that it has become a fashion, we almost infer that it has become so for no particularly good reason, and will probably shortly cease to be so for no better reason. The tragedy of this world is simply that because of a shifting moral sense, society forms its own rules and standards without regard or thought to the revelation of God in His Word, and in His Son Jesus Christ. Hence the Apostle admonishes us—be not fashioned according to the world, which has taken no thought of God.

II. THE DOCTRINE PICTURED

This is not a new picture, for we discover in the entire Old Testament that God has given us examples which are to be followed. He tells us in I Corinthians 10:11: "All these things happened unto them for ensamples: and they are written for our admonition. . . ." What then is the picture which God has painted of Israel in the Old Testament?

A. Separation in Custom (Deut. 12:29-31).

God commanded Israel to abstain from following after heathen customs and rites, and actually forbade them from even inquiring into heathen rites lest they follow them. The same picture is given to Israel again in Leviticus 18:29-30 in which the heathen rites are called "abominable customs" before the Lord.

It is true that Israel wandered again and again from the path established by God, but there can be no doubt that the very restriction was one of the things that kept Israel from falling into deeper sin.

B. Separation in Company (Deut. 7:1-6).

There can be no doubt that it was God's intent that this people was to be kept an holy people unto the Lord, and therefore He demanded that they should not violate their nationality with intermarriage, nor with treaties of any kind. God gives His reason for this when in Deuteronomy 7:4 He reminds them: "They [the parties in an intermarriage] will turn away thy son from following me, that they may serve other gods. . . ."

Again, it is true that Israel failed in the keeping of God's command, but it is likewise true that because of it they became a weakened nation. The one redeeming feature about it was that sufficient numbers of the people were willing to obey God so that He was always able to maintain a faithful remnant for His name's sake. It was only because of this that He was finally able to send His Son, the Lord Jesus, to us through the Israelites.

C. Separation in Conduct (Lev. 18:3).

Israel was likewise commanded to be a separate people in the matter of their conduct so that God through them could bless the heathen nations round about Israel.

As you study the tenth chapter of the First Epistle to the Corinthians, remember the history of Israel and know that it was done for an ensample for us. God led them carefully through the Red Sea, and watched over them in spite of their sin in the wilderness for forty years, and guarded them every step of the way so that their conduct might be holy and separated from the peoples of the earth. One of the most wonderful commentaries on the wanderings of Israel, and their conduct is that of the seventy-eighth Psalm. Israel was rebellious, and disobedient in their forty years of wanderings, and we read in verse 41: "Yea, they turned back and tempted God, and limited the Holy One of Israel." Yet God did not fail them, and brought them into the Promised Land.

III. THE DOCTRINE IN PRACTICAL APPLICATION

And now we come to the very practical application of this doctrine, as we think of nonconformity in these areas of custom, company, and conduct. The church must look back to Israel for the pattern of separation, but into the New Testament for direct word concerning our own age.

What Israel was able to accomplish in spite of her failures is but a small fraction of what the church should be able to accomplish in this generation of the Holy Spirit, if she will but heed the admonitions of the Word of God.

A. Religion.

The chief concern of God for the Israelites was that they should not adopt the customs of the other nations, and particularly the religious ceremonies and rites, lest these turn them away from worshiping and serving the true and living God. The same is true in our own church age.

The entire paragraph of I Corinthians 10:16-22 is a warning against the practice of idolatrous worship, for Paul reminds us that it is actually the worship of demons. We have moved first to this matter of *separation* in the things religious because of the current trend in our own day. Men are substituting things for Christ, and, while membership in the church is at an all-time high, attendance in the worship services of the church is dipping to proportionate new lows. Never before have so many belonged; yet so small a percentage of the population actually have gone to the services of worship. Why? We are allowing the religious rites and ceremonies of joining a church with all that accompanies it to become the substitute for true worship.

Perhaps we could say—everybody is doing it; that is, joining the church; therefore it is the right thing to do regardless of what change has taken place in the heart and life of the church member. This is a tool of the devil to steal the visible church from the Lord of the church. Paul speaks of it in II Timothy 3:5: "Having a form of godliness, but denying the power thereof: from such turn away." From such, keep yourselves separate.

B. Speech.

A second area in which we need examination in the matter of separation is in conversation, or speech. The New Testament is filled with admonitions and warnings concerning the speech of the believer. It is best summed up in the words of I Peter 3:10, where we read: "For he that will love life, and see good days, let him refrain his tongue from evil, and his lips that they speak no guile." But perhaps we ought to examine a bit more evidence to discover what is meant by "keeping the tongue from evil."

We shall only attempt to present in brief consideration a few of the passages that can be used to show God's hatred of an evil tongue. The Lord spoke against the "idle word" in Matthew 12:36. Perhaps we shall not know this side of heaven all that is included in this idea of "idle words," but let us remember that conversation that does not tend to the glory of God is but idle talk. Words are the only vehicle man has to convey his thoughts on any subject, and an idle word means an idle thought, and an idle thought is the tool of the devil just as much as idle hands.

Then in the fourth chapter of Ephesians, Paul warns in several verses concerning language. We are admonished to put away lying in every form (v. 25); and in verse 29: "Let no corrupt communication proceed out of your mouth." Christians should be careful of the words they use and the thoughts they convey to others. This verse alone ought to stop forever from the lips of any and every Christian the smutty story that carries with it the suggestion of licentiousness in any and every kind. And then Paul adds quickly in verse 31 a bit more concerning the speech of the Christian when he says: "Let all bitterness, and wrath, and anger, and clamour, and evil speaking be put away from you." What change would take place in the lives of Christians and in the church if everyone would be more careful of his speech, and even the tone of voice in the uttering of the speech!

C. Dress.

I know that this particular matter has been a subject of controversy in the circles of the church for many years, and there are extremes in application here that make a mockery out of that which God intended. However, God has said some important things concerning wearing apparel, and they ought to be taken to heart by those who are following God as His dear children. There is an Old Testament passage that bears upon the matter of dress, when, in Deuteronomy 22:5, God warns: "The woman shall not wear that which pertaineth unto a man, neither shall a man put on a woman's garment: for all that do so are an abomination unto the Lord thy God." Then, turning to the New Testament, He reminds us that "whose adorning let it not be that outward adorning of plaiting the hair, and of wearing of gold, or of putting on of apparel: but let it be the hidden man of the heart, in that which is not corruptible, even the ornament of a meek and quiet spirit, which is in the sight of God of great price."

Changing fashions in the matter of clothing are coming from nations that have forgotten God, and from designers that never knew our God. In talking with one of our African missionaries, I asked her concerning the matter of the dress of African Christians. Her only reply was significant. She said: "At least they never take off more after they have been saved."

If American men and women continue to move in the direction of the present, and Christians persist in following the custom of the world instead of abiding by the admonition of the Lord, we will be accepting the pagan custom of more and more nudity until it will no longer shock the moral conscience of our nation. A brief trip to the average beach, or a walk down the main street of an average town will show the direction in which we are headed. God warns against this!

D. Pleasure.

Many of the youth of our land somehow have the strange notion that to become a Christian means the end of all pleasure. Such is the very opposite of the truth. However, God does have some things to say about the kind and place in which we ought to get our pleasure. Read the words of Peter, in his first Epistle (I Peter 4:3-4), where he says: "For the time past of our life may suffice us to have wrought the will of the Gentiles, when we walked in lasciviousness, lusts, excess of wine, revellings, banquetings, and abominable idolatries." As you read the stories of the Old Testament, think of the number of illustrations that come to mind concerning God's judgment upon "riotous living." The generation of Noah was said to be one of reveling and pleasure. Jesus describes it in Matthew 24:38: "They were eating and drinking, marrying and giving in marriage." Sodom and Gomorrah were filled with riotous living and excess, and what shall be said concerning Belshazzar and the feast he made for a thousand lords in which there was feasting and drinking of wine and even the declaration of the "gods of gold, and of silver, of brass, and of iron, of wood, and of stone." Yet in it all, there are those who would follow the custom of the world in seeking pleasure with the things of the world. Let us again remember, there is nothing wrong in eating, marrying, giving in marriage, but the connotations of the passage indicate that it was that which accompanied the entire program.

E. Family Life.

God established the home as the very first institution upon the earth. He had set boundaries upon the home, and requirements for the home in both the Old and New Testaments. However, almost from the beginning of time, those laws of God have been broken, and men for every little whim have excused themselves in the breaking of the law.

One such demand of God in the relationship between man and woman is set forth in Paul's first letter to the Thessalonians (4:3) where he says: "For this is the will of God, even your sanctification, that ye should abstain from fornication." The tragedy of the hour is that the custom of the world toward premarital sexual relations is being accepted in many places as not only permissible, but actually that it is helpful as well. Our newspapers, magazines, books are filled with it.

The church has been quieted on the subject of marriage and divorce because so many of her members have adopted the custom of the world. Marriage, God says, is an honorable institution (Heb. 13:4), but marriage and remarriage either with or without divorce as established by Hollywood is an abomination to the Lord. A new study by the church on such great passages as Ephesians chapters 5 and 6 together with the letter to the Colossian church ought to be made in order that once again marriage might hold the high place that God intended it to hold. Jesus had sufficient to say concerning divorce in the Sermon on the Mount (Matt. 5:32): "But I say unto you, That whosoever shall put away his wife, saving for the cause of fornication, causeth her to commit adultery: and whosoever shall marry her that is divorced committeth adultery." Let the church again speak the words of the Lord, and let Christians everywhere stand by what God has said rather than by the customs of the world.

F. Social Life.

How shall the Christian behave himself in relation to other Christians, and with non-Christians? In his business, what shall be his attitudes and his actions? These are all a part of the matter of following of the customs of the day, or of being separated because of the fact we are Christians.

God has given answers in His Word, and we need to discover those answers. James 5:1-6 deals with the problem of labor and management, and the sum of it all is that even though he may suffer at the hands of the employer, he is urged to wait upon the Lord. Paul speaks of our actions in relation to dealing with a man business wise, when he says: "That no man go beyond and defraud his brother in any matter." Make the application to this as you are led, for it has to do not only with big business deals, but also with buying a bushel of apples, or trading a car. There are other matters that might be discussed in relation to our social life, but these must be reserved for other occasions.

IV. CONSISTENCY IN NONCONFORMITY (Rom. 12:1-2)

But how is all of this possible? Again, we turn to the statement of the doctrine and find the answer. The negative side of the picture has been presented. We are ready to look at the positive. "Be ye transformed, by the renewing of your mind." The word "transformed" describes a change in the outward manner of life that corresponds with the inner life that has come as a result of the new birth. With the Spirit of God dwelling within— imparting to the believer every virtue and grace of Christ himself—we ought to live that life in a public manner to the world. How is this accomplished? Paul answers: "By the renewing of your mind."

This is accomplished in just one way; namely, by learning and obeying the Word of God: "As a man thinketh, so is he." Men think, and if they allow their thinking to control their wills, then they make determinations that result in their daily lives. There are some men who refuse to think, and act only on the impulse of their wills, and, as a result, their lives are lived accordingly. As men think God's thoughts, they will begin to desire to live as God wants them to live, and they will begin to be transformed in their outward actions. This is what Paul meant when he said: "But we all, with open face beholding as in a glass the glory of the Lord, are changed into the same image from glory to glory, even as by the Spirit of the Lord" (II Cor. 3:18).

No wonder Paul said to the Philippian church, in Philippians 4:8: "Whatsoever things are true, whatsoever things are honest, whatsoever things are just, whatsoever things are pure, whatsoever things are lovely, whatsoever things are of good report; . . . think on these things." Ask yourself the following questions as you go over this list of things which Paul has suggested. Where do you find these things to think upon? In your daily newspaper? In the average magazine? In the common television program? Truth, honesty, justness, purity, loveliness, things of good report are all the opposite of the daily news, and of the average television program. Yet what is it that gets most of our time and attention? No wonder there comes the problem of a breakdown of society and morals.

But perhaps you will ask: "How can I obey?" How does the transformation take place? We are not left in doubt as to the power which is to produce the change. It is the work of the Holy Spirit. The change begins within; we must invoke spiritual power, power from on high. It will not be denied us if we seek it. "Ask, and ye shall receive" is the promise of our Saviour. We must not begin to try to correct outward habits until we have implored inward grace. We must believe that the Holy Spirit has taken up His abode within our hearts; hence He is willing to give us the strength to live by the will of God.

Paul describes people who are alienated from God when he says: "They mind earthly things." The real secret of a transformed life is a transmitted life—somebody else living in us, and that somebody is the Holy Spirit. It is He looking out of our eyes, giving His beauty to our faces, and His winsomeness to our personality.

But Paul concludes by giving us the motive for it all, when he says: ". . . that ye may prove what is that good and acceptable, and perfect, will of God." We are here upon the earth in training for our life throughout eternity. As we yield ourselves to His will, we are simply finding His will working in us, knowing that it is real for day-by-day living.

The Second Coming
of Christ

✱✱✱✱✱✱✱✱✱✱✱✱✱✱✱✱✱✱✱✱✱✱✱✱✱✱✱✱✱✱✱✱✱✱✱✱✱

CHAPTER THIRTEEN

THE CHAPTER OUTLINED:

I. The Certainty of His Return
A. Old Testament Prophecies
B. New Testament Prophecies
C. The Promise of the Lord
D. The Promise of the Angel

II. The Character of His Coming
A. The Rapture
B. The Revelation
C. The Day of the Lord

III. The Challenge of the Second Coming
A. A Purifying Hope
B. A Comforting Hope
C. A Motivating Hope
D. An Awarding Hope

SUGGESTED BACKGROUND DEVOTIONAL READINGS

Monday—The Meeting in the Air (I Thess. 4:13-18)

Tuesday—We Shall Be Changed (I Cor. 15:50-58)

Wednesday—Waiting for God's Son (I Thess. 1:1-10)

Thursday—The Blessed Hope (Titus 2:1-14)

Friday—God's King Shall Reign (Ps. 2)

Saturday—King Over All the Earth (Zech. 14:1-11)

Sunday—King of Kings (Rev. 19:11-21)

March 11, 1942, was a dark day for the freedom-loving people of the world. General Douglas MacArthur was ordered by his superior commander to leave the Philippines. The overwhelming forces of the enemy were sweeping in. In a very simple and brief statement this great soldier of the United States said, "I shall return." Two and one-half years later, on October 20, 1944, he broadcast to the people of the Philippines these words, "I have returned."

On another day, which for the disciples of Jesus seemed to be a very dark day, for the cross was looming on the horizon, Jesus said: "I will come again!" Someday, in the midst of earthly chaos, He will declare, "I have returned." Many exciting days are ahead of the complete fulfillment of that moment. Many questions are in the hearts and minds of men. We look at several of them in this study, as we discover what the Bible has to say about the return of the Lord Jesus to the earth.

I. THE CERTAINTY OF HIS RETURN (John 14:1-3; Acts 1:11)

A Gallup Poll taken in the mid 1960s concerned the return of Christ. Of those replying, 55 percent stated that they believed in the second coming of Christ to the earth, 31 percent did not believe, and 14 percent had no opinion on the matter. The opinions of men are interesting on every subject, but on this it will not alter the fact one tiny bit. As a matter of fact, God has already prepared us for such reaction, for in II Peter 3:3-4, He tells of scoffers in the last days: "Knowing this first, that there shall come in the last days scoffers, walking after their own lusts, and saying, Where is the promise of his coming? for since the fathers fell asleep, all things continue as they were from the beginning of the creation."

God answers these scoffers, for all things have not continued as they were from the beginning. There was a universal flood whereby the earth was destroyed (cf. II Peter 3:5-7). This flood can be demonstrated scientifically and Biblically.

What then gives us assurance of Christ's return to the earth?

A. Old Testament Prophecies.

The larger part of Old Testament prophecy is devoted to His coming in glory and power to destroy His enemies and to establish God's Kingdom among men. These are the prophecies to be fulfilled at His second coming.

1. Genesis 3:15 contains in seed-form the suggestion of both the first and second coming of Christ (Satan would bruise His heel) refers to His

first coming, while the second coming is seen in the fact that the woman's seed would bruise Satan's head.

2. Genesis 49:10 tells us that: "The scepter shall not depart from Judah, nor a lawgiver from between his feet, until Shiloh come; and unto him shall the gathering of the people be." The reference to the scepter and the lawgiver applies to the ruling, reigning ministry of the Messiah, which can only be fulfilled at His second coming.

3. Psalm 2, one of the Messianic Psalms gives us the introduction of God to His Son as His chosen King in spite of the conspiracy of the kings of the earth against His anointed. (See also Psa. 24, 45, 50, 69, 72, 110—all of which speak of this coming King and His kingdom.)

4. Isaiah 9:6-7 speaks of the birth of a child, the giving of a son, one called ". . . Wonderful, Counsellor, The mighty God, The everlasting Father, The Prince of Peace," upon whose shoulder shall be the government, upon the throne of David forever. In Isaiah 26:20-21, this coming is identified with the Lord himself.

These are but a few of many prophecies which look forward to the second coming of Christ in power and glory. Perhaps the culmination of Old Testament prophecy is that of Zechariah 14:4 where we read, "His feet shall stand in that day upon the mount of Olives." And then we read of the destruction of the enemies and the establishment of His kingdom.

B. New Testament Prophecies.

The New Testament is also filled with prophecies concerning His second coming. It begins with the promise of the angel as the announcement is made to Mary that she should become the mother of the Lord Jesus. The angel said: "He shall be great, and shall be called the Son of the Highest: and the Lord God shall give unto him the throne of his father David: And he shall reign over the house of Jacob for ever; and of his kingdom there shall be no end" (Luke 1:32-33).

Paul often gives promise of this as in II Thessalonians 1:7-10 where he promises . . . "rest . . . when the Lord Jesus shall be revealed from heaven with his mighty angels, in flaming fire taking vengeance. . . . When he shall come to be glorified in his saints. . . ." In I Timothy 6:14-16 he exhorts Timothy to faithfulness, ". . . until the appearing of our Lord Jesus Christ: Which in his times he shall shew, who is the blessed and only Potentate, the King of kings, and Lord of lords; Who only hath immortality. . . ." James and Peter add their prophetic voices to Paul and the Apostle John opens the final book of Scripture with the words, "Behold, he cometh with clouds; and every eye shall see him . . ." (Rev. 1:7).

C. The Promise of the Lord (John 14:3).

Not least of the prophecies concerning the second coming of the Lord is His own promise found in John 14:1-3, particularly the phrase, "If I go . . . I will come again. . . ." The Apostle Paul picked up this phrase as a basis for his teaching in chapter 4 of the First Epistle to the Thessalonians. It is at the second coming of the Lord in its first aspect that Jesus was promising, when He said, "If I go and prepare a place for you, I will come again and receive you unto myself. . . ." He did not promise to send another to bring us to Him, but rather, He promised that He himself would return and gather us unto himself. He will never be satisfied until every one of His redeemed people is with Him in the glory of His Father's house. He is there now preparing that house for us and, when it is all in readiness, He will return to receive us unto himself according to His promise.

D. The Promise of the Angel (Acts 1:11).

While the disciples watched, Jesus returned to heaven in what is commonly referred to as "the ascension." God sent a message from heaven through an angel who said, ". . . this same Jesus . . . shall so come in like manner as ye have seen him go into heaven" (Acts 1:11). The whole world listened as three American astronauts in outer space read the account of the creation of the world as it is recorded in the Book of Genesis. What a thrill it was to those of us who know that God did create the heavens and the earth. But here in Acts 1:11 is another message from the heavens. It was so important that God sent a messenger all the way from heaven to the earth, to say that Jesus would come again.

These promises and prophecies are so plain that any child can understand them. Why should intelligent men and women refuse to believe?

II. THE CHARACTER OF HIS COMING

In the Old Testament the promise was, "The Messiah is coming." In the Gospels this unfolds into two comings, and the promise is "Jesus is coming again." In Paul's Epistles this second coming unfolds into two aspects. First, He is coming in the air to catch away His saints. This is the Rapture of the Church. Then, after a period of time, He is coming in power and glory to establish His kingdom. This is referred to as the Revelation. We need to keep these two aspects clearly in mind as we investigate the Scriptures.

A. The Rapture (I Thess. 4:13-18).

Although there are frequent passages in the New Testament that refer to the second coming, this passage gives us a very clear picture of the first aspect, namely, the Rapture of the Church.

1. *The persons involved* (vv. 14-17). Two groups of people are involved in the Rapture. (1) The first group is referred to in verses 13 and 15 as, "them which are asleep," and in verse 14, "them also which sleep in Jesus," and again in verse 16, "the dead in Christ." The use of the word "sleep" is a term sometimes used in the New Testament to describe the death of a believer (cf. John 11:11-13). The Christians in the church at Thessalonica had apparently become disturbed about those of their group who had died, wondering if they would miss the participation of the blessed hope which Paul had taught them to expect. They were awaiting the return of Christ momentarily, but while they waited some had died. Now, Paul writes to give them comfort and instruction, telling them that those who have fallen asleep in Jesus will not miss the Rapture. As a matter of fact, "the dead in Christ shall rise first," coming out of their graves in an instant of time. (2) Then the second group mentioned in verses 15 and 17, "we which are alive and remain." This means that when Jesus comes back for His Church, there will be believers alive here on the earth. If Christ should come today, we would be among those who are alive and remain. If He tarries His coming, we may fall asleep in Jesus. But the Rapture, whenever it comes will include all of the true Church, those who are a part of His bride.

2. *The Lord and His involvement* (v. 16). The verse declares that "the Lord himself shall descend from heaven. ..." This is exactly what the Lord promised to do when He said, "If I go ... I will come again, and receive you unto myself ..." (John 14:3). Every writer of the New Testament refers to it, and every chapter of this letter to the Thessalonians talks about it. Jesus is coming again. We are told three things about it: (1) "With a shout." The word used by Paul suggests a shout of command, the loud, sharp order of an officer to his troops. Jesus used a visual demonstration of it in John 11:43 when He cried for Lazarus to come forth from the tomb. The word used here is even a stronger word, but it gives us the significance of this command. (2) "With the voice of the archangel." One archangel who is named in the Bible is Michael (Jude 9). According to the Book of Daniel (10:21; 12:1), Michael is especially the "prince which standeth for the children of thy people," that is, for Israel. So the voice of

the archangel here suggests that this is an event of great significance for Israel. Remember, with the Rapture of the Church, the church age closes, and God is again dealing with His people Israel. (3) "With the trump of God" is the third phrase of significance. In the Scriptures, the trumpet was used for two functions. First, a trumpet called Israel together for the worship of God, and the trumpet with other instruments of music sounded forth the praise of the Lord in the temple worship (Num. 10:2, 9). Second, the trumpet was used to call forth God's armies to war (cf. Joshua 6:4; Judges 7:16; Joel 2:1; I Cor. 14:8). To further strengthen this, there are the seven trumpets blown in Revelation, which seem to signify God's declaration of war and destruction upon the unbelievers of the earth at the end time.

3. *The events of the Rapture.* Three events are suggested in this same passage to the Thessalonians when the Lord comes for His Church. (1) We are told that "the dead in Christ shall rise first." We need to remember that when a believer dies, his body is placed in a grave, but immediately at death, his spirit goes to be with the Lord in heaven. Now at the Rapture, the souls of those believers who have died will come along with Him (v. 14). The bodies of these individuals will come out from the graves; their spirits will be reunited with their resurrected, glorified bodies; and as individuals they will go to be with the Lord—and the individual includes body, soul and spirit. (2) The second group involved is "those who are alive," and to get the full impact of this, we move to the great chapter on the certainty of Christ's resurrection, I Corinthians 15:51-54. Here, Paul reminds us that the dead must be raised with a new, glorified body. But, ". . . We shall not all sleep, but we shall all be changed." Twice Paul says it: "We shall all be changed" (vv. 51-52). He describes the transformation by saying that "this corruptible [body] must put on incorruption, and this mortal [body] must put on immortality." Just as the dead in Christ will be raised incorruptible, so the living will be changed into incorruptibility. (3) Then comes the third event, the catching up of all the saved to meet the Lord in the air. This is the source of the idea concerning the Rapture. The word rapture comes from the Latin, and means "caught up" or "snatched up." Having caught us up in the air, He takes us back with Him to heaven. Praise His name! One other great truth that Paul reveals about the Rapture is that it will be really very sudden. Paul says, "In a moment, in the twinkling of an eye . . . ." Everything in the present day is moving toward "instant" action. Here it is in the ultimate. The Lord will descend,

the shout of command will be given, the last trumpet will be blown, and instantaneously, without advanced warning, without preparation, without time for a countdown, the resurrection out from the dead, and the transformation of the living will usher into the presence of the Lord, all members of the body of Christ and at the same moment, the beginning of the terrible hour of the days of God's wrath on His enemies.

B. The Revelation.

The second aspect of Christ's second coming is reflected in the name used to identify it. We call it the Revelation to identify it from the Rapture. It is a scriptural title often used in the New Testament in referring to this event. The word means an uncovering, an unveiling, a making plain, a manifestation. Until this moment the world has been in the darkness of night. Satan has been blinding the eyes of them that believe not. God and righteousness have been real only to the eyes of faith. But in this moment of the Revelation, all will be changed. Until now, God and His ways, His kingdom, His people, His purposes have not been clearly seen or understood. Now, in the Revelation, these things will be opened up to plain view.

1. *The time of the Revelation* (Matt. 24). When the Lord began his great discourse about the things that were yet to be as recorded by Matthew, the disciples began to ask questions, and one of these at least is still with us, "when shall these things be?" (Matt. 24:3). We discover several things about the Revelation. (a) It is a secret, which God has not chosen to reveal. It will actually never be known until it happens. Many Bible students have attempted to set dates, but the Bible warns against this (Matt. 24:36, 42, 44; Mark 13:32; Luke 12:39-40; Acts 1:7; I Thess. 5:1-2, 6). (b) It follows the Rapture. From the day Jesus went away until the present moment, the Rapture has been imminent—it may happen at any moment. There is not a single prophesied event, not a single sign which the Bible puts between our own times and the Rapture. Christ's coming to take us to himself is the next event on the prophetic calendar. We are waiting and expecting Him to come at any moment. When the Rapture takes place, then Scripture outlines a series of events which will bring us to the moment of the Revelation.

2. *Signs prior to the Revelation.* Let us remember that the signs which Jesus gave to the disciples have to do not with the Rapture, but with the Revelation. After the Rapture takes place, there will be seven years in which the Antichrist will reign with power—the tribulation will be upon

the earth; Israel will return to the land; there will be a ten-nation confederacy; there will be an invasion by the enemy in the land of Palestine. When we speak of signs, remember that only as we see these things we know that the Revelation is getting near, and that means that the Rapture is closer by seven years.

C. The Day of the Lord.

The Revelation of Christ will usher in "The Day of the Lord," which is a technical name involving the millennial reign of Christ upon the earth. This Day of the Lord follows immediately upon the close of the Tribulation period. It will continue for a thousand years. It will be the fulfillment of the desires of men. The Old Testament prophets saw God at work in human history. They traced His dealing with the nations and warned of His coming judgment. When man's day is done and the Revelation takes place, the Lord Jesus comes to take over. The kingdoms of this world will become His kingdom. It will be the beginning of a golden age. The government will be perfect, justice will be done, the physical world will no longer be under the curse. There will be right moral standards, and it will be a world in which men will truly worship in spirit and in truth for the Lord God himself will be the just ruler. A very hasty trip through even one of the Old Testament prophecies will bring much light upon the character of the millennial reign of our Lord. In Isaiah 2:1-5 we read of the time when all nations will flow into the mountain of the Lord's house: ". . . and they shall beat their swords into plowshares, and their spears into pruninghooks: nation shall not lift up sword against nation, neither shall they learn war any more." Chapter 9 and verses 6 and 7 speak of the birth of the child, the giving of a son, and closes with this promise: "Of the increase of his government and peace there shall be no end, upon the throne of David, and upon his kingdom, to order it, and to establish it with judgment and with justice from henceforth even for ever . . . ." In 11:6 he continues: "The wolf also shall dwell with the lamb, and the leopard shall lie down with the kid; and the calf with the young lion and the fatling together; and a little child shall lead them." Reading chapters 32 to 35 of this same prophecy, and we discover the intertwining with the judgments many clear references to the glories of His kingdom and the blessings He will bring when He comes.

The other truth is that when He comes in Revelation, it will mean judgment upon sin and the sinner. The Old Testament foresaw this aspect of Christ's coming. In Malachi 3:1-6 the people were eagerly anticipating the coming of Messiah to free them from their yoke of bondage to foreign powers and bring them into the glorious kingdom. But the prophet warns them. After speaking of His coming in verse 1, he asks the question in verse 2, "But who may abide the day of his coming? and who shall stand when he appeareth? for he is like a refiner's fire, and like fullers' soap." The Lord is coming, but that coming will bring with it judgment upon sin.

III. THE CHALLENGE OF THE SECOND COMING

But prophetic teaching of all kinds has a deeper purpose than just to give us an insight into what will come in the future. The Lord gave us some very pertinent reasons for His teaching of these things, and Paul adds yet others, while John adds his voice to those already given.

A. A Purifying Hope (I John 3:1-5).

John reminds us that we will be like Jesus because we will see Him as He is. This likeness begins at our conversion, continues to grow throughout the life of the Christian, and is completed when we see Him at His second coming. But at verse 3, John makes the application, "And every man that hath this hope in him purifieth himself, even as he is pure." The hope of the coming of Christ, and our glorious future with Him is an incentive to us to live pure lives even as He is pure.

Jesus spoke of this when He taught concerning His coming in Luke 21, beginning at verse 34. There are at least four ideas regarding holy living presented in this one paragraph. (a) Simplicity in living—"Take heed to yourselves, lest at any time your hearts be overcharged with surfeiting" (dissipation). The entire passage has to do with the return of the Lord, and the events connected with it, and the way He urges men to be ready is to see that your hearts are not burdened down with a self-indulgent life, too much gratification of the appetites. In this day when the world is putting so much emphasis upon proper diet, perhaps we should once again suggest that the real reason for keeping our bodies in proper perspective, and not eating too much rich food is because the Lord Jesus is coming, and we ought to have our minds centered upon Him, and not upon food. (b) Beware of alcoholic beverages—"and drunkenness." I suspect many of you remember the sermons preached on the subject of temperance as it relates to alcohol. Here, Jesus urges His followers not to be drunk with alcohol at His coming. How little alcohol does it take to fog the mind so that you would not be thinking clearly about the coming of the Lord? (c) Then he adds "and cares of this life." The Lord is urging us not to be submerged in worldly cares, responsibilities and duties. There are many who would not think of overeating, or of getting involved in drinking alcoholic beverages, but who would not hesitate a single moment to get preoccupied with the cares of this world. There are business opportunities, the cares of the household, and the social duties of life. The Lord is urging, in light of His coming, that we do not get involved to the place of choking out the spiritual life. (d) Add to these the appeal of verse 36, to "Watch ye therefore, and pray always," and we discover yet a fourth element. The second coming is an incentive to a life of holiness that is undergirded by careful watchfulness and prayer. The Lord was preeminently a man of prayer. In the four Gospels, we discover at least twenty-five occasions when the words pray or prayer are involved as we read of His activities.

B. A Comforting Hope.

In John 14:1-3 Jesus said, "Let not your heart be troubled. . . ." The second coming of Christ is one which brings comfort to the heart of the believer, but, in addition, the Apostle Paul said (cf. I Thess. 4:13-18), as he wrote concerning the second coming, that we are to comfort one another with these words. The world is filled with a lot of sorrow, and there will be more and more as the days move toward His second coming. However, we do have a tremendous hope—He is coming again. We are to sorrow, but not as others who have no hope, and that hope is in the fact that Jesus is coming again, and will bring those who love Him to be where He is.

C. A Motivating Hope.

Then the second coming is a hope that motivates for service (Luke 19:11-13). In the story which Jesus told His disciples concerning the nobleman, it is quite evident He was showing them the coming kingdom. This would be postponed for a little while, but in giving direction for the interim He said, "Occupy till I come." The word translated occupy is a business term. It means to busy one's self, to be engaged in business, to make money by trading. Christ has left His business in our hands while He is away. In light of His coming, we must conduct ourselves as stewards of His business until He comes.

D. An Awarding Hope.

We are reminded that we are to look for His coming. This indicates not only a confidence that Jesus is coming, but it suggests an eagerness for His coming. It will be the end of our weariness and troubles. It will be the beginning of eternity with the Saviour. Hallelujah—what a Blessed Hope!